COLLECTED
ESSAYS OF
Robert
Bitzer

 DeVORSS *Publications*

ISBN: 0-87516-620-2
Library of Congress Catalog Card No.: 89-51300

Second Printing, 1994

DeVorss & Company, Publisher
P.O. Box 550
Marina del Rey, CA 90294

Printed in theUnited States of America

Dedicated to

MARGUERITE

my marriage partner of fifty years
—a great inspiration and a tower of strength—
for her faith, integrity, perseverance, and loyalty.

Contents

Many of these essays originally appeared in *Creative Thought* Magazine and the bulletin of the Hollywood Church of Religious Science.

Demonstration Milestones

I WOULD LIKE TO SHARE with you a few experiences that show how the Science of Mind worked for me and how I know it will work for you.

We begin with our major premise or belief: one Power—God, infinite Mind—holds us in its embrace of love. Its intelligence is unlimited and its ability to do is infallible, but it can only do for you that which you are conscious of being. The expansion is in your receptivity. It acts according to your belief. This is the key.

These milestones show various steps in the demonstration process to help you realize that what others have accomplished you too can do. Laws are no respecters of persons. Principles do not change to accommodate the individual. Not what you desire or feel you should have, but what you think creatively, determines what you get. There is no limit to the Principle; there is no limit in your ability to use it. Your beliefs can be changed. This is where your growth comes in. Your belief system, like your mental capacity, can grow. You are the answer.

My introduction to metaphysics per se came in a most unexpected manner. During World War I, I was a pilot in the American Air Force attached to the British forces. At one time I was a patient in the officers' ward of a British army hospital. I was experiencing excruciating pain. The medical doctors could not locate the cause, and their only thought was possible surgery.

The mail brought me a book from my father. It was H. Emilie Cady's *Lessons in Truth*, which I had never seen. At random I opened to a paragraph which said that intense criticism and emotional disturbance could produce great aggravating pain. This seemed to fit my case.

In an adjoining bed was another American officer who was loudmouthed, uncouth, and obnoxious. I was greatly disturbed because I felt he was giving the British the wrong impression of the Americans. As I read the paragraph, the pain stopped instantly. Without understanding the details of what took place, in letting go of the criticism I came into the possession of a different attitude. This changed attitude toward the sick fellow-officer released the bitterness and criticism. It freed me from irritability and pain. What a discovery!

After serving overseas for almost two years, I decided to continue my education. There was no GI Bill of Rights in those World War I days, but the way began to open. I went to Columbia University with the intention of preparing to enter the College of Physicians and Surgeons, but infinite Mind began working in ways that I had never heard of. My father, who was a practicing dentist, was interested in the Truth. He heard that Dr. Frederick L. Rawson was coming from England to give some lectures in New York City, so he came up from Virginia, and I went to hear Dr. Rawson with him.

This was my first lecture and it almost became my last. Dr. Rawson had broken with Christian Science and had established a world-wide following of his own. Rawson told that as he was walking down the street one time, a man in front of him slipped on a banana skin. His feet went higher than his head, but he did not touch the ground. Rawson "reversed" the situation, and the man regained his equilibrium without touching the ground. That was straining my belief. However, I could believe it now. I have seen things perhaps more miraculous than that; I have seen all kinds of conditions healed. The law of "reversal" works.

I knew Dr. Rawson had *something*, so I began to investigate in New York City. Every Sunday morning at the old Waldorf Astoria at 34th and Fifth Avenue, Dr. W. John Murray filled the spacious and elegant Grand Ballroom with a capacity audience. His teaching expanded my consciousness immediately.

For instance, from earliest childhood we had cards at Sunday School saying *God is Love*. I had taken it as a matter of course, meaning little. Dr. Murray said the same words, *God is Love*, but something different occurred. The old belief in a God

4

of wrath and condemnation became a God of love and under-standing and revealed the truth about man. God was Presence, real, whole, life, health, and prosperous being. The people that sat in darkness had seen a great light.

This was the Church of the Healing Christ (Divine Science). Years later Dr. Emmet Fox became pastor of this church. My experience there was a great mind-stretcher. In the rotunda at the entrance to the ballroom was a booktable. Books by Dr. Murray, Elizabeth Towne, Emma Curtis Hopkins, and many others were sold. Imagine selling books in church, and on Sunday at that! I was really undergoing a metamorphosis. My adjustment was quick—each Sunday I made a beeline for the booktable. I learned how to use affirmations and denials and began to help people through positive prayer.

About this time two of my friends who had served in the war became sick, and both died. Rumor had it that they had not received proper medical attention. However, when I visited Virginia, all those reports were refuted. These men had received the best medical attention available. Immediately my reaction was: it was not right for these friends to die. If medical science had done all it could, then there must be a higher power that could have saved them, and I resolved to find it. This was the start of my healing ministry.

I began to study with Mary Etheridge Thompson Chapin. She was a Radcliffe graduate—a stately, statuesque woman over six feet tall. I called her The American Beauty. Her opening affirmation every Sunday morning was:

I am the open channel through which the healing currents of life are now flowing. God is my life; God is my health; God is my success; God is my perfect being.

Mary Chapin was known world-wide as a lecturer and healer. An aunt of mine living in Washington suddenly got spinal meningitis. She was past sixty-five. Mary Chapin made a trip to see her and my aunt was healed. In Great Britain Mary Chapin had worked with Judge Thomas Troward. Judge Troward paid great tribute to her. He said, ''I do the teaching, but Mary

5

Chapin proves it through her healing work." She had great praise for Troward and always made me feel that I knew him. In 1926 she served as president of the International New Thought Alliance, whose annual Congress was held in New York that year. Indeed, New York was the place of my spiritual birth, just as Bethel was the place of Jacob's spiritual birth.

I found another group in New York City at 222 West 72nd Street: The League for the Larger Life. It was similar to the Metaphysical Club in Boston, where the transcendentalists got together, also like the Metaphysical Club run by Edith Buck in San Francisco. These centers offered a platform to visiting metaphysicians—traveling speakers who would stay a week or longer giving classes and lectures, then move on to New Thought Centers from city to city. I served as secretary of the League, meeting many of the truly great.

Once one of our regulars, Harry Gaze, was eating in a restaurant a few doors away. The waitress asked, "Do you wish for a cup of coffee, sir?" Gaze replied, "My God, do you have to *wish* for it to get it in this place?" So I got another great lesson in how the principle works: It's not what we wish but what we *know* that demonstrates. Gaze was an Englishman; a brilliant, dynamic speaker. His lectures always seemed short. His success secret was short, dynamic talks. Always send your audience away satisfied but still wanting more.

Another prominent speaker at the League was Dr. Orison Swett Marden. He was a prolific metaphysical writer whose books sold almost four million copies and were translated into twenty-eight different languages. He was well known as the publisher of several "Success" magazines. When I gave my first lecture in New York City, he was president of the League and attended, offering me great encouragement. Other great speakers were Eugene Del Mar (founder of the League), Mary Allen, Maude Pratt Messner, Emma Curtis Hopkins, Dr. Alfred Grier, Brown Landone, William Andrew Bahre, and Jessie Boerstler.

About this time one of the "giants" of New Thought came to the League—Julia Seton, M.D. She had been a practicing

6

physican in Iowa. As a contributor to the *Journal of the American Medical Association*, she began writing articles about how the mind helps heal the body. As she continued to write, her articles became bolder and bolder on the power of the mind. The AMA stopped accepting her articles, so she decided to go full-time in metaphysics. She filled one of the large Broadway theaters with a series of Sunday morning lectures. She founded the Church of the New Civilization and established branches all around the world. She was a very dynamic speaker, over six feet tall and standing very regal.

When she was ninety-six she spoke for me at the Hollywood Church of Religious Science. She was asked if she would live her life differently if she had it to do over. She replied she would do everything that she had done, only it would not take so long. For instance, instead of being married to Sears, her husband, for seven years, she would have finished it in seven hours. On one occasion she was speaking at a summer seminar at Oscawana-on-Hudson, outside of Peekskill, New York. Sears interrupted her. When she objected, he said, "But dear, we are one." She retorted, "Yes, I know, but *I* am the one!" When she spoke for me in Boston, I extended my arm to escort her to the pulpit, but she turned me down. She did not need an arm. She was truly a woman of the New Age.

When Julia Seton spoke for us at the League, she told me that a church she had established in Boston needed a pastor; would I be interested? I accepted the call from the Boston church. Several people offered to help finance my move, but I refused to borrow; nor did I want to take money from my family. I depended upon divine Principle. I had no idea how it would work, but it did. One week before I was scheduled to leave New York I received a letter from my father. Enclosed was a check for my share of the sale of timber on the farm in Mississippi of which I was one of the heirs. I did not even know that there was any salable timber on the farm. I depended on divine Principle. The check from the sale of the timber was more than enough to take care of my move.

The group in Boston was small. They had Sunday afternoon services, which I switched to Sunday morning, and the congregation began to grow. After about a year I wanted to visit my family in Virginia. William Andrew Bahre, one of the traveling teachers, was lecturing at the Metaphysical Club. He was unable to speak for me but said, "Ernest Holmes is in town. Why don't you ask him?" I said I did not know him. Bahre said, "He is a friendly individual and very approachable."

When I called on Holmes at his hotel he said that Dr. Seton had spoken for him, and that he would be glad to speak in one of her churches. Holmes first met Seton in New York. He was waiting for her in the lobby. When she entered the lobby he went forward to meet her. She said, "How did you recognize me?" He replied, "Your feet were the first feet coming in that door that knew where they were going"—a key to the acumen and intuitiveness of these two giants.

By the time I returned from Virginia, Holmes had already left Boston. Later, when he returned, I visited him to thank him. From that time on we became very good friends. He gave a series of classes in my Boston church on Mental Science. His class had four lessons, and the topics were *The Thing Itself; What It Does; How It Works;* and *How to Use It.* The lectures later became the first four chapters of his famous textbook, *The Science of Mind.*

Although Ernest Holmes was in town on business, he spent most of the day dictating metaphysics. Neither one of us was married at that time, and we spent the evenings reading what had been transcribed during the day. It was my privilege to read the entire manuscript before it went to the publisher as the original edition of *The Science of Mind.* This was before Religious Science had been formed. We traveled a great deal, and Ernest spoke at New Thought centers in Manchester and Concord, New Hampshire; Providence, Rhode Island; Springfield and Worcester, Massachusetts; and many other places.

When I was living in New York I had seen an advertisement for "The Holmes Brothers"—Ernest and Fenwicke. However, I had never heard of them. Fenwicke was what we called a traveling psychologist at that time. After Dr. W. John Murray passed on, Fenwicke was pastor of The Church of the Healing Christ in New York City. He was a prolific writer, a polished scholar, and an orator. One of his books, *The Law of Mind in Action*, is still an outstanding work.

As my friendship with Ernest grew, we planned that I would return with him to Los Angeles, where he had lectured at the Brack Shops, the Ambassador Theater, and other places but had no regular established work. He left Boston rather hurriedly, and I could not get away at that time. Upon his return to Los Angeles, his book went to the publisher, and he began to establish permanent headquarters. His Sunday morning services at the Ebell Theater were soon filled to capacity. With offices on Wilshire Boulevard, The Institute of Religious Science and School of Philosophy, Inc. was born and established.

In the meantime, Ernest married a very prominent woman, Hazel Foster, who became a great power in the work. Our friendship and our desire to work together had grown stronger. On St. Patrick's Day, 1930, I got a letter from him in which he said he felt that Hollywood would be a wonderful place to have a branch of his movement, so in that same year I opened the first branch of the Religious Science movement. After sixty years I am still there.

Except for Christian Science and the Unity School of Christianity, the metaphysical movement was very lacking in cohesiveness when Ernest Holmes first came on the scene. The International New Thought Alliance was an effort on the part of the many independent schools and movements to get together on some kind of a united basis. Its origin and purpose was to bring all these leaders of centers, as they were called, together in an annual congress. It avoided favoring any one group. It offered no classes. Since 1914 it has been holding annual conventions in the principal cities of the United States, Canada, and Great Britain.

Emma Curtis Hopkins, who had been with Mary Baker Eddy, separated and formed her own school. She became known as "the teacher of teachers," having taught Charles and Myrtle

Fillmore, who founded the Unity movement; H. Emilie Cady, writer of the Unity textbook, *Lessons in Truth*; Elizabeth Towne, publisher of *Nautilus*, the first metaphysical magazine to appear on newsstands from coast to coast; Ella Wheeler Wilcox, one of the most famous poets of her era; Annie Rix Militz, who co-founded the Home of Truth; and Ernest Holmes, who studied privately with her in New York City.

Nona Brooks, co-founder of Divine Science in Denver, was one of the first leaders to own property and build a great edifice. The original New Thought leaders generally held their services in hotel ballrooms. Brooks would not permit her group to build until they had all the money necessary. She resisted pressure and stuck to her principle—no debt. The Divine Science church in Denver is still one of the most impressive in the field.

Ernest Holmes recognized the need for cohesiveness in the teaching. He was a very clear thinker—a philosopher rather than a priest. He recognized that a movement could be only as strong as the literature that supported it. He had published two books prior to the *Science of Mind* textbook: *Creative Mind* and *Creative Mind and Success*. Both had been very well received. He started a monthly magazine, *Religious Science*, which was soon changed to *Science of Mind*. Its slogan was "Helps You Help Yourself."

He also organized a program of study that attracted students from all over the United States. He was quick to recognize the power and prestige of the University of Southern California and the University of California at Los Angeles. He had some of the most prominent professors from these universities speak in his Major Course. This lent creditability and prestige as well as a curriculum that was interesting and exciting. As Dr. Holmes continued to write, the Religious Science movement continued to grow. Its churches are in the hundreds and are worldwide. It is a major metaphysical movement of which we can all be proud.

Many of the most prominent and influential people in the movie industry were interested in Science of Mind. Theda Bara and her husband, Charles Brabin; Doris Kenyon and her husband, Milton Sills; Marie Dressler; Harold Lloyd's mother, who gave many art objects to the Institute of Religious Science; J. Farrell MacDonald; Beulah Bondi; Ethel Clayton; Mae West; Jeane Wood; Ruth Stonehouse; Adela Rogers St. Johns; Robert Young; Peggy Lee; Mickey Rooney—these are among many names that could be mentioned. And Goodwin Knight, while Governor of California, occasionally spoke at the Institute on Sundays.

The background of my experience in Hollywood has been varied. When I arrived in California in 1930 the Holmes family lived on eight acres in Palms. Ernest and Hazel lived in one house at the top of the hill with Ernest's father and mother, Hazel's mother, and a cousin, Adela Chadwick, who was also one of the practitioners at the Institute. In another house, Ernest's brother Guy lived with his wife and family. In still another house lived Ernest's favorite niece, Josephine Holmes Curtis, and her husband. Eventually Ernest and Hazel sold their home to Adela Rogers St. Johns.

Adela had been a long-time friend of Hazel. She had arranged a double date: for Ernest and Hazel, and for Fenwicke Holmes and Gussie Rundel. That was the start of the romance between Ernest and Hazel. When Ernest and Hazel moved to a mansion in the Wilshire district, they kept a permanent guest room for Adela.

I had met Ernest's brother Guy when he was in Boston with Ernest. One evening I was visiting them in their hotel suite and Guy slumped out of his chair onto the floor unconscious. Ernest and I sat by him on the floor, treating. Pretty soon Guy came to and we resumed our laughing and chatting, but this did not last long. He had another heart attack. I asked Ernest if I should call the house physician. He replied, "Just treat." Presently Guy recovered and did not have another attack for over twenty years. (Again our dependence on divine Principle had been proven.)

Dr. Holmes was a warm, friendly individual—very gregarious. His family seemed to revolve around him. He was very strong, level-headed, and always a tower of strength to them all. He was very "home" conscious and loved to cook. When he was fifteen he cooked, using a 150-pound barrel of flour each day at a lumber camp down in Maine. He did not have a lazy bone in his body. I would sometimes drop in on Saturday afternoons, and it was not an uncommon sight to see a roast in the oven, a ham boiling on top of the stove, and maybe a couple of burners going. At the same time he might be running the vacuum in the living room. However, most of the cooking was done next door in Guy's house.

Reginald Armor, whom Ernest had trained as a practitioner and a minister, was practically Ernest's adopted son. Reg, his wife, and son lived on the hilltop adjoining the acreage in Palms. It was Reginald that pushed hard for branches of the Institute. He took it on as a special project. In the beginning Dr. Holmes had not envisioned branches. He was not interested in a religious movement. He preferred to have an institute and not a church. However, in continuing to hold classes, the graduates inevitably created platforms of their own. Gradually Ernest accepted the idea of churches. All of a sudden he began to envision churches nationwide, all with the same architectural design. That idea never materialized.

Ernest also contemplated all churches having the same topic and sermon each Sunday morning. That was tried out. When I was head of our ministerial group, which had a luncheon meeting each Monday, I would get Frederick Bailes to give the ministers a suggested outline for developing their sermons from the same topic. Dr. Bailes was one of the most brilliant speakers we had in the movement. These lessons in homiletics were a tremendous help. Dr. Bailes gave a radio talk after the ten o'clock nightly news. When people complained about the late hour, he replied that he did not want in his Sunday morning audience people who went to bed by ten. He was a super salesman with a medical background.

In the early nineteen-fifties, our luncheons had grown to around thirty ministers each week, but they had never organized. Dr. Holmes, who attended every week, requested me to appoint a committe to organize the group, primarily so that it could be self-disciplining. In due time it became the International Association of Religious Science Churches (IARSC), whose membership consisted of the Institute of Religious Science and its existing branches.

About that time, I announced that I was going to Europe. In itself, that was no big deal. I had spent two years there in the AEF during World War I—but this was to be no ordinary experience; it was to be different. How or in what way I did not know. I spoke my word and released it.

My demonstration came in a strange way. In September 1949 the INTA held its congress in Dr. Ernest Wilson's church in Los Angeles. He was president but did not want to serve another term, so Dr. Raymond Charles Barker and Dr. Ervin Seale approached me separately and asked if I would be interested in serving as president. At the first Board meeting after I had been duly elected president, I stated that if the INTA was going to use the name *International*, it should function as international. (That it had not been doing except in 1914 at a congress held in London, where it had adopted the word *International*.) Responding to my comment, Dr. Barker moved that "Dr. Bitzer, our president, be sent to Europe."

So my trip got under way. I held to my major premise: I depend upon divine Principle for my work, my health, my supply and my good. My conscious mind could not possibly have planned all the things that were to happen. When I arrived in Stuttgart, I was met at the airport by the governor; the superintendent of the airport; Mr. Hans von Kothen, publisher; Mr. K.O. Schmidt, prominent author; news reporters from Reuters; and a charming lady who presented me with an armful of red tulips. This was ample proof of my positive consciousness: Know what you want to do but do not outline how it is to be done. Spirit is all-knowing.

Prior to World War I, Mr. von Kothen published the strongest monthly metaphysical magazine in Germany, *Die Weisse Fahne*. K.O. Schmidt was the editor. Mr. von Kothen arranged my German itinerary. Both of these men were interned during

13

the war because of their anti-Hitler protests. Fortunately, they were able to bury their typewriters and presses so that as soon as the war ended they were free to resume their publishing. Among the books which they had published was *The Prophet*, by Kahlil Gibran, in German translation. They were a powerful group and worked ceaselessly to halt the Nazi abuse. We worked under the handicap of different languages. However, the German trip proved to be a great help to the New Thought groups there. It helped unify our teachings. At that time Munich was still in ruins and many bombed buldings had not been excavated. I spoke in English to a large crowd in the auditorium at the Munich Museum. Our message was timely, and it was warmly received.

From there I took a tour bus to Berchtesgaden. I did not speak German, and the driver spoke no English. We stopped for a coffee break and I tried to order a Swiss cheese sandwich and a Coca-Cola, but I could not make my wants known. A young man with a very attractive girl came up to my table and offered to help. Afterwards, at every stop they took me under their wing. At Berchtesgaden we had an opportunity to get acquainted. The young man worked in the photographic business in Wiesbaden. He had planned to drive to Munich, pick up his girl friend, and continue the outing to Berchtesgaden. At the last minute he had car trouble, so he proceeded by bus with his friend. They were the answer to my demonstration.

In turn, I was the answer to their demonstration. At the Cologne Photo Exposition he had met a friend of mine, Mr. Joseph Dombroff, who was the owner of New York's Willoughbys, the largest camera store in the world. The young man intimated he would like to move to New York. I offered to speak to Mr. Dombroff when I returned to New York. In relating this, Mr. Dombroff said that he would gladly spend $25,000 as an investment in the young man. Divine Principle had completed its action. No one was imposed upon. All gave freely and generously, and all made a complete demonstration. Needless to say, the young man went on to become a great success in the field of photography. Later, he appeared at the Hollywood church with his bride.

I made several trips to South Africa. On one trip from Rome, my flight went over Kimberly. I had always wanted to see the "great hole" there. Divine Principle demonstrated it. Dense fog at Capetown compelled us to land at Kimberly, where we spent the night. The next morning the pilot circled the great hole, flying low—an amazing and unbelievable sight. Later in the flight we circled Mt. Kilimanjaro, the highest peak in Africa. Dr. Hester Brunt, a relative of South African prime minister General Jan Smuts, had established a strong center in Capetown. I helped her get a new Science of Mind center started in Johannesburg. Despite the terrible unrest, we have had courageous leaders in South Africa who stick to the Truth, among them Dr. Hester Brunt, Dr. Vere Wilson, Dr. Naomi LeRoith, Dr. Linda Clark, Dr. Sheila Szczawiski, and Dr. June Jones.

My next destination was Paris, and again the demonstration was made by ways and means that I knew not of. I was met at the airport in Paris by Mr. Welles Bosworth with his private limousine and chauffeur. He was known as the Rockefeller architect and was architect for the Massachusetts Institute of Technology. He was the only American architect to be a member of the French Academy. (He had been commissioned by the French government to restore the Palace of Versailles.) He drove me to my hotel and then to the apartment of the Sterlings for luncheon. That evening I spoke for Dr. Mary Sterling and her audience of 1500 people at Unité Universelle. I had sent my manuscript ahead for her to translate into French but gave my lecture in English. She repeated the lecture in French.

Dr. Mary Sterling and her American husband, who was a practicing physician in Paris, had gone underground during the Occupation and were active workers. She did not have Sunday morning services, but their major activity was a class one evening a month held in a theater with fifteen hundred or more students. Additional activities were conducted at the center, Unité Universelle, throughout the week. Her French was fluent, without accent. She published a monthly metaphysical magazine in French, *Unité*. She ran articles in French by our principal teachers from around the world. My official visit seemed to open the way for others: Dr. Raymond Charles Barker, Dr. Ervin

15

Seale, Dr. Joseph Murphy, Dr. Raymond Holliwell. Dr. Sterling published my *How to Make Your Mental Computer Work for You* in French, and it had excellent sales. She also published books by many other Americans. She has been the metaphysical light of Europe. Her center became like a metaphysical highway with so many speakers going back and forth. We also had Dr. Harry Gaze coming back and forth from Great Britain. Brother Mandus at Liverpool had made a deep study of Science of Mind. I was instrumental in bringing him to the United States, where he made many trips across the country. The INTA had become international—another important milestone. I had depended upon divine Principle. It always works.

Several years later at the INTA Congress in Los Angeles, a stranger came up to me. She said she had set up in business several nephews in Sweden, but she felt it was time that they began to do for themselves. She put up a large sum of money for me to take New Thought to Sweden. I had no leads, only the money; but I found help in Stockholm—advertising, public relations, theater, ushers. In fact, all details were taken care of, and I put on a series of five classes on Science of Mind for about 500 people. All Europe is hungry for metaphysics, but it must be presented in a scientific way—and as the science that it is.

Coming back to Ernest Holmes: he never got over the idea that the conduct of the churches should be governed by the churches themselves. Where disconcerting or contrary ideas were introduced, he felt that the churches should discipline their own members. Astrology, numerology, psychic readings, psychological group analysis therapy, automatic writing, reading tea leaves, and channeling were contrary to basic Science of Mind and should not be allowed. The confidentiality of the practitioners and ministers must be kept inviolate.

Dr. Holmes was a terrific practitioner. Sometimes he would sit on one side of the desk facing the student; sometimes in a chair away from the desk. Sometimes his treatments would be entirely silent; other times they were audible.

He was an inveterate scholar. Often when we were traveling together in New England we would read a book out loud—

16

for example, Sir Edwin Arnold's translation of the Bhagavad Gita. When we encountered a word that we were not familiar with, we would have to stop and look it up. (With all the Sanskrit that goes with the Gita, we had quite a task.) That was Ernest's nature and explains why, although he had less than eight years of formal education, he became a self-educated scholar who was able to include Dr. von Kleinschmidt, president of U.S.C., and Dr. Robert Millikin of the California Institute of Technology as peers. This also explains the many degrees that he received.

Dr. Holmes had studied Blavatsky's *The Secret Doctrine* and the works of Aurobindo. Although he was never a member of the Christian Science movement, he knew the textbook, *Science and Health*, almost by heart and could quote Mrs. Eddy. He had studied with the Leland Powers School of Expression in Boston, where Mrs. Powers was Second Reader of the Mother Church. In fact he felt so sure of the teaching that he put a shingle outside his office: "Ernest Holmes, Christian Science Practitioner." Of course they made him take it down. He never lost his respect for Mrs. Eddy and his love for the teaching. I believe this had a great influence on his work. The Mother Church idea especially influenced him.

From my earliest relationship with Dr. Holmes it became very clear that he assumed a personal responsibility for everything that happened to him. We were having lunch at a very nice place in Boston, but the service was slow. He spoke up, "Someone at this table believes in procrastination." No condemnation—but never admitting to the existence of a cause outside ourselves. I carry this a step further: procrastination is subconsciously creating delay because of our belief in unpreparedness.

One of the most important ideas that Dr. Holmes added to the thought of the time was that of definiteness. Prior to this, the movement lacked definiteness. Students and teachers sat around waiting for Spirit to tell them what to do or to cause things to happen. Science of Mind stresses we are surrounded by a universal Mind that is creative by nature. It accepts what we

17

think into it and causes our thought to happen. He developed a technique of treatment, or scientific prayer, based on our thought, such as: "There is but One Mind, God, or Spirit, everywhere present in its entirety of being."

This power becomes to us what we believe when we believe that it becomes to us what we believe. Each of us is the creative center of his or her own individualized universe. The success of our method depends upon our complete dependence upon our spiritual mind absoluteness. Thus we do not touch the person for whom we are giving the healing. There is no laying on of hands, no manipulation or massage; no emotional touch or embrace. The work can be done silently or audibly. The practitioner can sit at a desk with the student opposite or in a chair away from the desk. The thing to remember is, no physical contact. Otherwise you are getting into physical vibration, and you will break your spiritual mind contact. Remember, it is *consciousness* that heals.

One time, when Dr. Holmes gave me a long silent treatment, I asked what should I be thinking. He replied, "Anything you want to think; I am giving the treatment." On one occasion Hazel Holmes was doing some treatment work for me. After she finished I asked, "Now what shall I do?" She smiled and did not answer. I repeated my query. Finally she said, "Did not anybody ever tell you to let the practitioner do the work?" She also had a Christian Science background of study and was an outstanding practitioner.

As a student of metaphysics and later as a minister, I had a very fine relationship with the leaders in the field. The dedicated student soon discovers there are no inferior people and that there are no superior people. There are just people, and they become to us what we think. Emerson said, "When you are in the presence of greatness, you too are great." God in me is one with God in you; one Mind, one Spirit, one Life, one God. This is the key to getting along with people. Maintain your consciousness on the God level and do not deviate from that. Critics tried to convince Winston Churchill to do the opposite. They urged him to be all things to all people, to meet them on their own level, take up their weapons, fight fire with fire. The great diplomat replied, "Let me see you sting a bee." When you depend on divine Principle, you never stoop to any person's level but bring all experiences up to where *you* are.

No matter what you are attempting to do, always get the vision before you begin to work. See the completed demonstration. If you are buying a house, think of it as fully furnished and completely paid for. Even though you may take out a mortgage on it, treat that it is completely paid for. For the first property our church bought, we worked that way. Instead of waiting twenty years to pay off the mortgage, we did it in eight years.

When we got ready to build our new edifice, we contemplated methods of financing. Churches have a peculiar risk: no bank wants to have to foreclose on a church because of the bad feeling involved. One of the largest banks wanted every member of our Board of Trustees to sign the note, personally guaranteeing the loan. If any signer defaulted, the loan would have to be instantly absorbed by the other members. That I would not permit. I depended upon divine Principle.

While we were treating, one of our members accidentally ran into a friend who was on the Board of one of our banks. He asked the man if his bank would like to lend the money for our proposed new building. Without a moment's hesitation he said, "Sure. Come around to the bank." We got the money we needed, and again we paid off the mortgage in half the time. From the beginning, we had the consciousness of the church being built according to our specifications, completely furnished and fully paid for.

I wanted a new three-manual organ. I had studied organ and at fifteen I organized a thirty-voice choir and became its director and organist. In our new church a group of several people wanted to put on some entertainment to raise money with which to buy the organ, which at that time cost only $25,000. I said, "No, the organ is going to be fully paid for before it is installed," and it was. I depended upon divine Principle.

I do not believe in potluck dinners. Ernest Holmes also was against them. He said a person gets a five-dollar dinner for a dollar and a half and runs around saying he gave five dollars to the Lord. Neither do I believe in mounting entertainment or other affairs to raise money. Depend upon divine Principle. I believe that the church should be financed through tithes and gifts. We give generously to our source without the expectation of a reward. This is the law of prosperity. A farmer holds back one-tenth of his crop for the next year's crop. We give our tenth or more, recognizing the source and substance of our supply. Another way of looking at it is that we are priming the pump.

When our beautiful new edifice, the Hollywood Church of Religious Science, was completed, we decreed that nothing used should go into it; all things must be new. The church is not a dumping ground for castoffs. We give God our best. The minister is not subject to charity. He has a responsible position to fill and must hold his self-respect high. The church is not a charitable organization. It is a nonprofit religious educational corporation.

When I was a student at Columbia I did some tutoring. One of my jobs was teaching a ten-year-old boy on Long Island. I was met at the train by a driver in an old-vintage open Ford. I wondered if they could afford me. Of course they could, but I kept thinking I was overpaid. Well, my word has always been the law, so I was informed that the school that this boy attended required all coaching to be done by accredited members of its own teaching staff. So my word worked(!)—but I admit I felt relieved.

As for money: I have never worked for money. I depend upon divine Principle. I have never experienced lack, because I know the source of my supply. I never depend upon the channel but only on the source. I am open to all avenues through which my good comes. I thank everyone who is an instrument and show my appreciation, because no one *has* to be a part of my demonstration. However, the source blesses and prospers everyone that it uses. Understanding this law, we are never imposed upon, nor can we impose upon someone else. Bless everyone through whom your good comes. I have always been governed by this law—long before I ever heard of metaphysics.

The greatest milestone in demonstration was when Marguerite Van Horn and I were married. She was a successful business woman and a well-oriented student of our teaching.

Immediately she brought a new impetus of power into the work. She had a deep understanding of Principle and a clear insight into how a church functions. From the very beginning she has been a great inspiration and a tower of strength. For the almost fifty years of our marriage she has stood shoulder to shoulder with me and has been a tremendous power in the activity of our ministry of healing. She is fully ordained and is one of the most powerful practitioners that I have ever known. She has not wanted to go on the platform, but her dynamic presence has made itself felt in other ways.

Prior to our marriage, I had carried full responsibility for the church. I paid all expenses necessary to get the work started out of my own pocket. We had never been endowed. Although I started the first branch of the Religious Science movement at the request of Dr. Ernest Holmes, I had never received any financial help. Dr. Holmes did not believe in financing a new minister. He felt that the minister must do it on his own. If he had it, he would make it. Well, I made it. I depended upon divine Principle. Now we decided to transfer the responsibility from my shoulders to those of a board of directors. This took the work out of the purely personal, and we incorporated as a church. This was another milestone.

There is no limit to the future of metaphysics, but there is much uncertainty regarding many of the present organizations. The future depends upon the individual effort. Metaphysical organizations have already begun to decline. Their effectiveness will finally be measured by the individual effort. The basic principle of Science of Mind is inexhaustible. Where the groups bring in various extraneous ideas such as crystals, channeling, automatic writing, psychic group therapy, the work is weakened. By way of contrast, the early pioneers were strong-minded leaders who were not afraid to tackle anything. They were known as spiritual mind healers, not practitioners. All cause was within their consciousness. They bore the brunt of skepticism, ridicule, and unbelief, but they were dauntless.

The movement will rise or fall according to the individual use of consciousness. We shall demonstrate what we think in

21

consciousness; not what we desire or want. Principle will never let us down, and we shall never stop using it. Understand its laws, the way it works, and never doubt or deviate. Metaphysics has already changed the way life is unfolding. Computers and related technologies are but one example of basically *metaphysical* progress. Mind has made all these advances, and mind goes beyond all appearances, or physical phenomena. It programs right mental and spiritual activity within you. Your challenge becomes your opportunity, and your opportunity becomes your demonstration. It is in this way that I regard the future.

As we teach people how creative Mind works and how to depend upon divine Principle, they recognize that all cause originates in mind, limitless in ability and possibilities. Organizations come and go. I have seen it happen over and over again. The power is within you, not within the organization. You depend upon Mind—God, or Spirit. It is done unto you according to your belief. The group, whether it be the state, the church, or some other organization, cannot take the place of individual creative thinking. To try and push the responsibility onto the group only weakens your grasp of the Truth. Within you is the power. Beware of placing your allegiance outside yourself. You are the only future. You are the result of the choices that you make. Place the power where the creativeness is. You are the answer. What is the question?

Basic Principles I

Basic Science of Mind

SCIENCE IS THE revelation of principles and laws that govern the universe. You may not know why they work in certain ways, but you know that they do. From a physical point of view, the beefsteak and potatoes you eat are turned into fingernails and other parts of the body. It remains a great mystery. Your happiness reflects itself in your face. So does your discouragement or depression. Your courage and faith generate tremendous energy and cause you to be active. What you feel and think acts on your physical being. How? You can go a step beyond this. You can cause what you think about to happen. Why? Because a law is involved.

You find the same mystery in nature. For instance, you plant a bulb in the soil, and it becomes a beautiful lily. How? Does the soil act on the bulb or the bulb on the soil? You don't know; it could be both.

A friend wanted to plant five acres of spinach. The nurseryman showed her a new variety which he thought would be wonderful. She said it looked like carrot seed to her. She listened to the nurseryman against her better judgment, and her crop came up carrots. Your desires and actions must be consistent with what you want. The Law is definite. Failure thoughts produce failure even though you wanted success. It takes spinach seeds to produce spinach; carrot seeds to produce carrots. It takes a success consciousness, which thinks only success, to produce success. Your subjective mind does not know that you want success until you think success. Then the Law gets your command and produces success. Does this seem preposterous or strange? Do you think the tomatoes that the soil produces are a miracle? Of course not. It is the Law at work. There is a law that acts intelligently according to a principle.

Mind seems to have two distinct functions. For instance, you have discovered a subconscious mind that is subject to your conscious thought. Under hypnosis the patient is commanded to act in certain ways and he or she does. The conscious mind of the hypnotist bypasses the conscious mind of the patient and commands the patient's subjective or subconscious. The patient does what he or she is told to do. What a wonderful world this opens up. You do not have to accept experiences that come to you; you can do something about them. Your subconscious can reject that which is incompatible. You do not have to be an average individual or accept the run of the mill. Instead, you can create the kind of world you want to live in. You can change your thought and think creatively what you want.

The interplay between conscious mind and subconscious mind is comparable to the action between the bulb and the soil. These observations have revealed the two functions of mind—conscious and subconscious. You have discovered a law. Consequently, what you think about yourself with conviction, you become in your expression. The conscious mind chooses; the subconscious executes. What you think, you become. Thus you discover for yourself that Mind is a science.

Get this first step clearly. You are a creative thinker. You can give definite directions to your creativity. You are a conscious creator using a law that responds. You accept your new creative power.

The Power Source

SCIENCE OF MIND postulates only one creative power, Mind. Scripture states "In the beginning God." The gospel states "In the beginning was the word and word was with God and the word was God." These concepts converge. One Mind, one Principle, one God operating through the Word. God Mind expresses through your thought at the level of your understanding. You think the thoughts of God. You partake of universal power; its force is activating you as you. You start with First Cause—limitless Intelligence, Mind that knows. The power of your thought comes from this Mind principle. The Mind that conceived you endowed you with the same power to create.

Just as the soil in one yard has the same creative potential as the soil in the next block, so all individuals use the same creative Mind. The soil is not creative because it is your soil. It is creative because it was made that way. This same principle is true regarding your mental creativeness. It is not creative because it is your word. It is creative because it was made that way, but it becomes creative to you when you use it.

Your power is universal; it is not exclusive. All people use the same power. A small boy watching another boy swim suddenly realizes all boys can swim. It is a universal ability. All can use it. Your ability to control your life is not due to some dispensation of a divine providence existing outside yourself but is the application of power within you.

Universal Principle exists regardless of how you use it. "The thing that makes you sick is the thing that makes you well." Thought can make you sick or make you well. Thought can restrict you, limit you, and even make you poor. Your thought can prosper you and make you rich. The principle of Mind responds to your desire. God plays no favorites. There are no chosen sons and daughters who are exclusive, no chosen race, color, or sex. The rain falls on the just and the unjust. The sun shines on all alike. Each has access to the Infinite, and God can never be depleted by your activities.

The point is, while you are using a tremendous force, you are not invoking a power for special favors. This Mind includes health and happiness for everyone—just as the atmosphere is available to all, but each person does his own breathing. God's good is available to all, but each person must appropriate what he desires.

You accept or reject. This has to be a conscious act. All good is for all of us. As you turn from self-denial and self-depreciation, a tremendous force of power seems to rush to meet you. It takes longer to get sick than it does to get well.

You are dealing with a principle that is creative by nature. You are using a principle of success that is present everywhere. The law of growth is universal. Within the seed is the power of its own germination. Within your thought is the power to make it come true. Spirit has endowed all its creation with its own creative power. You do not have to make your thought creative. Principle has already done that.

Right Placement

A UNIVERSE OF ORDER would imply everything in its right place. This would apply to each of us. Right placement is part of the divine pattern. How do you recognize your right place? You do not use right as opposing wrong. Wherever you are is the right place determined by your thought pattern. Certainly the universal Mind would not have you live in a particular city on a certain street, nor would it imply that certain people had to be lawyers or teachers or sales people. You are an individual with the right of choice. You can be anything you choose, and you can succeed in anything, provided you comply with the nature of the law involved. The great singer developed her voice through practice. The great attorney studied his law books and case precedents and developed the skills necessary to win.

Your right place is developed along your lines of studied effectiveness. Success is not a chance experience but one of practice and skill. Success is your attitude of greatest effectiveness. Your vision, your desires, your inclinations and your skills make you effective. Your world is your thought objectified. You are a center of intelligence in an infinite Mind. This is the first step in effectiveness. Mind is inexhaustible. So are your possibilities of using it. You draw on this reservoir. You get from it the ideas you need and the ability to use them. You develop the conviction that you will always have the ideas that you need when and as you need them. This is right action and this is right placement.

What you shall do with these ideas involves the choice and decisions which you have made. You are rooted in this sustaining, ever replenishing system of Mind in action. You always hold the initiative because you are individual. You act first; otherwise you would be a puppet. Working from this inner Mind, you will always do the thing that will give you the results you seek. Your choice of mental material will match your overall decision. You are doing what you decided: that is what makes it right.

But suppose you decide to change your direction. You can always change your course of action, but not your method of creating. Life proceeds from the inner to the outer. The same Mind and Intelligence makes the lawyer or the salesperson. The difference is in the direction you give to the Intelligence. There is only one Mind, but you think it into the form you desire to experience. The Mind that keeps you well is the same Mind that keeps you prosperous. Your specific thinking is the difference, and that is what is important.

From this it is obvious that your right place is a state of mind rather than a location in space or time. You live and move in the one Mind and think it and act it into expression. You do not have to be in any specific place or do any particular thing. This Mind is wherever you are and in whatever you are doing. You are always in it and always have access to its informing and creative power. You are inseparably linked with it. That is what is meant by right place. You are in the stream of creative consciousness.

Consciousness

CONSCIOUSNESS, LIKE ANY other principle, can be used in a positive or negative way. In these studies you are using it only in a positive way. You are to be conscious of the truth. You are to be success-conscious. You are to be conscious of right action. It is necessary to be conscious of something definite or specific. To be conscious of nothing would make you unconscious.

Consciousness works on specific ideas. The success consciousness involves specific concepts. The money consciousness includes specific amounts. Success is a broad term that needs to be interpreted according to the individual's need and desire. A two-room apartment or a twenty-room mansion each could represent a person's idea of successful being.

The millionaire is not necessarily more successful than a person in a lower financial bracket. His or her focus is different. This depends upon a person's conditioning. Each is using the same Principle. Each is expressing his own idea into Principle at the level of his thinking. Each can hold or increase his consciousness of prosperous being through changing his awareness.

If a person lets up on his continuous aliveness, he might experience a seeming slump. This explains why success sometimes seems to go up or down. Nothing has happened to the success principle. The principle does not change, but the individual relationship can change.

The success consciousness must be fed. It must be stimulated. Your success idea of last year may be obsolete. Today requires new vision, new methods. The self of you requires a new sense of values and expansion of self-awareness. You need a new incentive and greater initiative.

You can increase your consciousness of good. There is nothing wrong with you where you are, but life is constantly challenging you to develop new talents and abilities. You do not

31

grow through comparing where you are with where you were a year ago. You grow through new ideas that absorb and overflow into a larger new expression. Consciousness is the key word. Not what you have, but what you are aware of being or having. You want to consciously know who you are, consciously recognize what you are doing, and consciously recognize and accept your personal expression.

This is a true mental/spiritual faculty that creates as it moves forward. Many people may miss an opportunity, but opportunities are repeated again and again. This is why you train yourself to recognize and accept. You become so absorbed in what you are doing at present that your consciousness is blind to the new idea trying to break through. Certainly what you are merits your full support and attention. You still need the openness to new ideas. You need to be consciously ready.

The new spell-binding project will not come to the indolent nor the person who is satisfied in believing that he is doing all that he can. It will come to the busiest and most active who knows he is always ready for a new step in consciousness. He anticipates beyond his present predicament. The successful individual working at his apparent peak has the consciousness that will carry opportunity beyond this moment. You go to the busiest person you can find, the most successful person. This is the law of consciousness. Unto him who hath it shall be given. A success consciousness attracts success. That is why the principle works.

Be Big

YOU ARE SURROUNDED by many beautiful things, most of which you take for granted or accept in a cursory sort of way. You accept them without giving them any deep meaning. You are apt to have that same attitude toward great truths. You give lip service but miss the deep meaning that would revolutionize your life. Mind is all. God is the only power. God is love. You could go on and on. You know the commandments, the axioms and aphorisms of truth. You can recite them by heart. However, to prove these truths and live them makes a greater demand upon you.

You are surrounded by a principle of wealth which is imploring you to accept it and use it. You need a personal commitment. Emerson said that if he took unto himself all the beauty which surrounded him he would surely give it out again. He identified with the beauty of the mountains and became part of what he was beholding. That is what is meant by consciousness. You are surrounded by prosperity and great good. Consciousness reaches out, recognizes what it beholds, accepts it and makes it part of your being.

This develops a new terminology. You are surrounded by limitless good. You can affirm you have abundant wealth. All of that can be true. You have all these potentials of being, but you must use them. This is where consciousness comes in. Having all wealth and all health does not necessarily imply that you are taking advantage of what is included for you. A definite creative step is necessary. You have abundant wealth and you work mentally to have the consciousness of what you have. You create the consciousness of abundance and acquire the consciousness of prosperous being. That will do the trick. You get the consciousness of having it.

Consciousness is the key to demonstration. It opens your mind to limitless possibilities. You do not merely affirm what you have; you affirm that you have the consciousness of being

33

successful. Someone may be waiting for you in your reception room, but this would not imply that you knew they were there. Consciousness connects you with the fact or the truth of being.

You are, in your experience, what you are conscious of being. The whole universe is yours, but you can appropriate only according to your consciousness. "All things that the Father hath are mine"; but it is obvious that you can actually have only that of which you are conscious. From this you can see that you should treat not merely for what you want but for *the consciousness of being* what you want. You live in a world of great beauty and you can become conscious of this. Limitless abundance is yours, and you can become conscious of what you want. Consciousness identifies with your good and makes it part of your being.

Infinite Mind knows no limitation and manifests according to the law of consciousness. You are limited by your belief, but you are not limited by Principle. Your potentials are inexhaustible, but your consciousness is the determining factor. You have a little or a lot. The Infinite does not care and does not restrict. Bigness brings consciousness forth; smallness contracts. You are big.

You, Yourself

You can be whatever you desire when you understand the law of creative action. You are versatile in your ability and can develop those talents which you consider desirable. You have certain aptitudes. The exotic or esoteric; the artistic or the mechanical; the scientific or business. No power outside of yourself has placed you in a specific channel, and there is no force that is trying to compel you to be a certain way. Your parents and early childhood may have made strong impressions, but you resist all outside attempts to dominate you.

You are a free individual. Since you are Intelligence operating intelligently, you don't put your choices in a hat and pull out one to follow. Nor can you be advised by a soothsayer or psychological counselor. You have to learn in your own way what is involved, what opportunity is afforded you. It is your life, and you are the only one that can live it. You don't let somebody else try to live it for you, and you don't try to live somebody else's life. You cannot do what you do just to make somebody else happy. *You* are the one to be happy. Your life is at stake. Trying to fill a position or profession just to make someone else happy never works. It results in a deplorable mixup.

Each person is self-contained and each alone knows what brings gratification and satisfaction. This inward awareness is not visible to the outsider. No one will ever really know you, and you will never really know anyone else. The more you abide by these rules, the better you will get along with people. The strength of this inner integrity on the part of two people is the basis for love. Right relationships are established by people who stand strong in their individual completeness.

The right to determine your freedom of expression must be extended to others. The Law always works two ways: what comes to you and what goes from you. You claim your privilege of freedom and extend the same courtesy to others. Whatever

35

you choose to be should involve research, study, and preparation. The principle of growth develops skill. The athlete undergoes rigorous training. The mystic spends many hours in meditation. The student of the Science of Mind works to develop consciousness. Trained thinking is more effective than scatterbrain thinking. These lessons show you the creative Mind at work and how you use the Principle each day.

There is no time element involved. The consciousness is developed each day through treatment and meditation. All power is in your thought. You constantly refute the suggestion that you are subject to things outside yourself. Your thought is the creative cause. What you think about yourself becomes your expression. You give no power to the situation you find yourself in. You are a self-contained center of limitless power. Your consciousness causes things to happen. You believe in the sovereignty of the self. You accept and reject. Your power lies in what you accept. The universal Mind is not concerned with what you do not want. It wants to know what you do want. It acts upon that.

Power-ful Decisions

DECISIONS GIVE LIFE its meaning. Your growth is the result of your conscious decisions. They represent how you are directing your creativeness. Adjusting yourself to situations over which you have no control does not bring spiritual growth. Such experience would develop tolerance, patience, and forbearance; but it merely accepts the status quo and disallows your opportunity for conscious choice.

Since you have discovered the creative Mind, you have to assert conscious control. Your power to make decisions is a definite step forward in your personal evolution. Up to this point of your spiritual awakening, the principle of evolution more or less governs. Nature is directing the evolutionary force to produce the self-conscious individual who takes charge of his or her personal life. Your experiences are intended to prepare you for this creative event.

Mass suggestion, mass production, and mass direction take care of your needs. The law of averages is the keynote: the survival of the species, the preservation of the type, and sustaining the race consciousness. All this changes when you become a self-conscious creator. No longer can the law of averages apply. The race consciousness has done all it can when you become aware of your individualized expression of infinite Spirit and accept your self-awareness. Everything changes. You are no longer *done* unto; now, instead, you *do* unto.

Life will manifest your self-choices. You choose what you want and demonstrate your ability to live with your choice. Your choice denotes your spiritual discrimination. What you think is important. Your basis of choice is not one of comparison but rather making a personal commitment. For instance, in choosing a house—Early American, French Country, Georgian, Tudor, or Colonial—it is not which is the "best," but which will adequately portray your desire. Which is better for dinner—steak or chicken? Again, you do not compare but take the one that appeals to you at the moment.

Your choice immediately gives you freedom and at the same time limits you. That is part of the growth process. You choose the road you want to travel and put all of your attention on driving it. You avoid wondering what a parallel road might look like and if it would have been better. You make your choice and stick to it. Your choice will fulfill the decision it involves as you keep your energy focused on what you are doing.

Your choice gives your direction its creative power. The purpose can never be overlooked. "Choose you this day whom ye will serve." No choice is forever but only for the period of aliveness in your desire. Life will continually let you complete your project and pursue another. Choice is more of a way and path than a goal and objective. The end of the trip is the beginning of another. Your attitude, faith, and perseverance bring the growth.

The power to comply with your decision is within the actual choice itself. Once you have chosen, you can fulfill. Do not let yourself waver. If the going gets tough, don't indulge in regret. Reconnect the power at the decision-making point. Remove the seeming obstacles. The greater the knowingness at the decision-making point, the greater the momentum in your demonstration.

Demonstrations
Are Exciting

WHEN YOU GET a new car, you can hardly wait to drive and show it off. Anything new presents a challenge and affords great excitement. This is true of new discoveries that you have made about your creative power. Driving your new car can be an ecstatic experience. So can your solo flight as an air pilot. These experiences will never be duplicated.

The same thing happens when you realize your new mental creativeness. You suddenly realize you don't have to take all the gaff you have been taking, nor can you be pushed into the background and watch those around you being promoted. You begin to move up. Your new self-assertion will begin to pay off.

But a word of caution: Do not be premature in telling others of your new-found power. You are the one to be impressed, not the world around you. Through the law of consciousness, you make sure your personal self-acceptance is complete. You build your inner strength and think yourself into the power seat.

Here is where you see your law of subjective mind come in. Your self-acceptance now acts upon the subjective mind. In the face of deep-seated convictions of inferiority and self-depreciation, you begin to affirm the truth of being—your new ideas, your ability, your worthiness, your efficiency, your stability, your dependability. As you make these new statements about yourself, you begin to believe them.

But your new self-discovery reveals an ally. Your subjective mind becomes your sponsor. It causes you to believe what you want to believe about yourself. At the same time it erases the old beliefs you want to discard. What a wonderful thought—and it truly fills you with wonder. Your life is important to the universal Life. You are a mover of the universal Energy. You are really a somebody.

39

When limited thoughts appear, you affirm that they have no power over you, and you believe this. Negative thoughts do not appear to test you. There is no temptation in the one Mind. The negatives come up in order for you to destroy them. You give the doubts no power and they fade away. You are not afraid of them. You are not backsliding. These negatives have been years accumulating in your subjective, but that does not mean it will take years to get rid of them. A person may take years getting sick but can be healed instantaneously. It takes longer to construct a building than it does to demolish it with the wrecking ball.

Your word acts swiftly as your commitment to your new discovery is completed. Your results in treatment can be phenomenal. You learn to think from the creative level. Your self-awareness governs you. You are cause to your world of experience. Your mind power is supreme.

You heal yourself of unbelief. Your poise can establish mental stability. You can get rid of indecision and uncertainty. You break the habit, through your use of mental law, of picking on yourself and others. Any thought or feeling can be changed. Any situation can be rendered harmless. Mind knows no obstruction. It knows only to be what it thinks and wants to be. This stand by you produces the power. You are unlimited Mind.

Control Thought

OUR UNIVERSE OF MIND is governed by principles and laws. These sustain order and work harmoniously. You are part of this universal being. You individualize this infinite Mind. The point of contact with this unusual force is in your own awareness—the sum total of what you call the self, what you are aware of being, from a personal point of view. The self does not include frustrations and controversies. Such ideas may seem to overwhelm you at times, but they exist only in your belief, and such beliefs are false. A constructive force governs the Universe. The same is true of the individual. You are reborn into a world governed by spiritual Mind. You are not your physical body, you are spiritual being. You function in a world of Mind.

As Mind individualized, you sense your true worth and reach out with infinite possibilities. What you can be is limitless. This staggers your imagination. The Self individualized finds itself at the center of the universe. What you think about yourself finds a higher level. It is not based on what you see surrounding yourself but on your inner world, in which Mind is the creative factor.

Your mental, spiritual perception becomes your world. This is positive, affirmative Mind in action. You show great respect for what you are. Your creative consciousness becomes sacred. You are expressing the Divine. Profane feelings and negative, derogatory feelings cannot exist here. You are the image of the Divine. You are a center of power. You genuflect before this inner self of you. You proclaim your true worth and release your unharnessed creativity.

This self-awareness is more than a casual thought or flashing image. This idea must grasp your entire being. You have to let it permeate your whole life. "In Him we live and move and have our being." You use affirmative statements of Truth.

"I am centered in the One Mind."
"God breathes into me the breath of life and I am a living soul."
"All the love, wisdom, and intelligence
of infinite Being have established my dominion."

Negative thoughts about yourself must be repudiated. False beliefs that made you feel and act self-depreciating, negative ideas that would destroy your divine birthright, give way to your new positive God-conscious acceptance. You assert the positiveness of your being. Where fear was, you bring forth faith and courage. Your new consciousness of the creative self becomes self-assertive. You are spiritually aggressive in the truth of your being.

To maintain this consciousness requires definite ideas on your part. Your thinking causes you to move forward in a field of Mind. Your creativity projects new action. Just as the rudder is operative only as the ship moves, so your vision functions only as you are active.

You cannot remain inactive. Subjective mind must move ahead. You let conditions around you take on the meaning of your inner contemplation. You move from the inner awareness to its specific action. Energy follows thought. Your ideas are power units. Definite things happen.

Inseparability of
Cause and Effect

ORDER INVOLVES THE RIGHT creative sequence. The cause precedes the effect. The thought precedes the thing. You work at what you want to be, and as you establish this in consciousness, the experience follows.

Subjective mind accepts your conscious thought and works on it, giving it form. Your subconscious mind can store ideas within itself and release them at some later time. This is why thought control is so important. You must not accept thoughts that you do not want to express. You reject unwanted thoughts the moment they appear. You block out that which is undesirable. You affirm there is nothing in you to attract negativity. Through the law of correspondence you draw to yourself that which will be like your thinking. Basically, you are good—the image and likeness of the Divine. You can reverse negative trends any time you desire. Your treatment can dissolve the negativity.

You can change any effect by changing the cause. The cause and effect are inseparable, and you should think of them as always being together, like the two ends of a dachshund. When the head moves forward, the tail goes along with it. The cause and its effect move together. This eliminates a waiting period. You can speak your word and expect immediate results. The cause and effect are one, but the initiative is always with the cause. Effects do not instigate action. They follow the cause.

Your environment is an effect that surrounds you. It has no power over you. If confusion seems around you, you change your thought. The cause, whether you consciously created it or let it pass unconsciously, is within your consciousness. You heal the condition by coming to terms with the self. You establish peace and harmony within yourself. Peace at the center brings peace at the circumference.

43

The causative law works in all that you do. Success is a state of mind that causes your business to prosper as its effect. You treat the attitude, not the condition. This is why you cultivate positive, affirmative attitudes of well-being. You create confidence in yourself. You believe in your ability.

Your consciousness of money determines your wealth. Money is an effect that outpictures your idea. You demonstrate at the level of your conviction. You are one with the principle of supply. Affluence is a state of mind that produces the money according to its concept. You should be specific when you are treating for money. When you write a check, you state how much you want. The law of Mind works the same way. Learn to be specific. This gives your creative power direction. You can always go beyond what you specify as long as you have given your thought its direction.

Expect your thinking to come to pass. Think what you want to happen. The law of cause and effect is very simple and very sure in its working. Keep your sequence. You live in a world governed by order. Be sure you know this.

Directing Consciousness

SINCE ALL IS consciousness, there must be definite ways in which it can be developed. To develop body consciousness, the athlete would go to a gymnasium. He or she would follow a rigorous training course to develop muscular strength and skilled performance. The thinking is directed toward the fulfillment of each bodily performance—a mental dexterity complete with knowing that something happens as muscles are coordinated and skill is directed. The mind really does the work, with its attention focused on fitness/performance. The Olympic games and competition reveal inexhaustible accomplishments, with no end to the challenges.

Money consciousness is another facet that you develop. It affords opportunities as endless as those in body development. As in the physical, all thought and energy is devoted toward what you want to see, so your concentration is on what you expect to see develop and not on what you have now. In the money consciousness, your mental action is positive and affirmative. The money pattern requires keenness of perception and alertness. Just as the gymnast is commanding muscles and nerves and telling them what to do, so the financier is commanding Mind substance to obey his or her thought. The money consciousness responds in the same way that the body does. It has laws which you can use. Money and its demonstrations are part of the consciousness.

But as important as these concepts are, you are seeking a deeper meaning. The above illustrations center on what you are doing. All these actions are subject to change. You can switch to an emotional consciousness or an art consciousness. Your major attack in any of these is upon your outer world, which you know is a world of effect. This is what Plotinus had in mind when he said that man is an amphibious being able to function on an inner or outer plane. But whichever the plane, he identifies with whatever is on that plane. This does not give you the

45

answer, for it remains a form of duality. You are unified being—one God, one Mind, one Life, one Cause.

You can easily see that the body-money-art consciousness represents effects, not causes. They are points of focus. So you look to Mind. Now your quest for consciousness assumes a different direction. You discover an inner awareness not dependent on anything happening or expressing in your outer world. That is your original being: first cause—the image and likeness. This comes as a great revelation. You do not repudiate or deny the wonders in your outside world, but you now meditate on the power that put them there. You are not dominated by your creation nor enslaved by your experience. "I created it and caused it to happen, but I am not my body nor my money. Then who am I?"

That answer only you can give. Moses called it I AM. It is the great mystery. You are the creativity of God. This comes only through deep meditation. Find out who you are independent of what you are doing in your world of expression. You are pure being—dependent on nothing outside yourself for completeness. This is ultimate consciousness.

The Ultimate

THE EASTERN ASCETIC sometimes has a tendency to negate his outer world. He becomes so engrossed in his spiritual experience that his outside world seems nonexistent. This would revert to a belief in duality. The Science of Mind student lifts his or her world or outside consciousness to the level of inner thinking. There is one Mind and one Substance. This becomes the focus of your spiritual consciousness. You use the same dexterity, the same keenness of approach that you used in developing a strong physique. Only now it is directed inward.

All creation is in Mind and is dependent on an expanding awareness. Spirit creates by becoming what it creates. You follow the same pattern. You become what you think. You develop the awareness of being the perfection: no separation between you and your creative power.

Ernest Holmes developed a wonderful technique of spiritual mind treatment which enables you to change conditions in your outer world. No other metaphysical system has been so thorough. Treatment and meditation deal with consciousness. They travel in your inner world of thought. This is where you find your identity and learn to be what you are. It is obvious that this inner world deals with quality of being, with mental/spiritual concepts. This is where you function as divine being.

Maintain your identity as spiritual Mind. Function in a world of form (outside). You are in it but not of it. Never identify with the condition, whether you call it good, bad, or indifferent. You are conscious mind moving in a world of creation. Ideas and things have no power over you. You create circumstances and situations, but they have no power over you. You can take them or leave them but never accept them as yourself.

Whatever attributes of being you think of as God you incorporate in your being. You can know God, or Spirit, only through like attributes in you. You can know God only at the level of your dominant consciousness. God becomes to you that which you believe God as being. Your personal belief must correspond to what God is. Thomas Troward gave as God's attributes Life, Love, Power, Peace, Joy. Meditate on these. The apostle Paul said whatever things are of good repute, think on these things.

This is your answer. Meditate on the quality of spiritual awareness that you want. Let it develop throughout your being. Life becomes your livingness, your flexibility. Power eliminates all weakness; love eliminates hatred and bitterness.

In the final analysis, you can know only that which you have the necessary equipment to accept. Only the happy one can understand joy. Only the one free from distrust and hatred can know what love is. Strength meets strength. Inner knowingness destroys uncertainty and produces only right answers.

The one Mind knows no division, no separation. Be at peace; you are not divided. You are one with the One. Meditation will give you your power. Follow it.

Basic Principles II

Check Your Vision

VISION IS AN IMPORTANT factor in your progress. It is creative action within the great Law. It is creative action looking ahead. Dreaming either looks backward at what has happened or lives in a make-believe world of imaginary satisfaction. Vision, on the other hand, sees your idea as creative action causing things to happen. The dreamer should turn his dream into specific action. "The old dream dreams; the young have vision."

Sometimes when you come indoors on a bright day your eyes seem to take a little time to adjust. This is also true of the dreamer. His imagination is so strong he has to adjust to what he is actually seeing. The dream wants to be seen as real. This is where the dream gives way to vision, and vision moves into action. The desire was already in objective mind just as the objects were already in the room you have entered. Vision always is creative action. In other words, stop dreaming of what you would like to be or do and see your vision as already being it. Stop dreaming of all that treatment is able to do and get the vision of what your treatment is doing now. You have dreamed and talked about it long enough. Act out your vision.

Clear vision is free from impairment. The mystical third eye was in the top of the head and was never closed. The vision that you have established is eternal seeingness. No matter what surrounds you, only that which you see is included in your experience. A magnifier brings your object closer to your vision. Your mental treatment acts in the same way. It is not so much creating new conditions as it is creating your vision to see it. What are you seeing? That depends on your direction. First, God—Good—Wholeness. See your source of being. This can never change. See you, yourself. Don't let psychological advice deter you. See the perfect you.

51

1. *See* the *Self* of you in action.
2. What you *see* in mind you can *see* as your objective form.
3. *See* yourself expressing creatively.
4. Give power to what you *see* yourself doing.
5. *See* Spirit in perfection action.

Your vision leads the way and you follow. Vision requires definite concepts. The psalmist said the people raged furiously because others had imagined a vain thing. Vision success—*you* as success. Extend this vision. Remember it is already established in your consciousness, but your vision has to see it. Only with your eyes can you behold the beauties and wonder.

Be definite in seeing what you want to see. Make your project complete in mind. With each delineation of thought, *see* your word as already existent. The single eye can see only good. You are creative vision, and you see yourself expanding. See your mental expression into the new idea. The farmer ploughs his field, getting it ready. This is his dream. Then he gets the creative vision and sows his seed. Only right seeing can bridge the seen and the unseen. Only your vision enables you to act creatively and make your dream become real to you.

Order

WHEN A THING functions and does what it was designed to do, it is in order. When any function breaks down, it is out of order. The connection with its source idea must be restored.

People get out of order the same way. Sickness and poverty result from broken connections. Health, happiness, love, and prosperity belong to the individual who functions in order. You were designed that way. Your mind and your consciousness must maintain self-control. You must act from consciousness. That is where the cause is. That is where the changeless design is. The inner you knows this and must be self-assertive.

The first step in preserving order is right sequence. Thought, whether it be conscious or subconscious, causes you to act. To break this sequence causes you to function out of order. Its symptoms could be sickness or financial depression or discouragement or doubt. An effect is never the cause. Your predicament or condition is not the cause of what happens to you but is the effect of what your thinking is doing. It is never the result of what someone has done for you or to you, whether it was good or bad. It represents what you have done to yourself. You are out of order because you are trying to convince yourself that effects are causes. You alone are cause. The idea comes first; its expression follows.

To keep yourself in order, you must generate new concepts and plans. Machines are constantly being improved because people are constantly generating new ideas. The horse gave way to the train and the automobile. The ocean liner gave way to the jet, and rocketry outpaces itself. All because your consciousness cannot stand still. You live longer and better.

The Science of Mind shows you how. You do not have to stay in one place. You have the ability to be what you want. But you must be sure you function in order. A new demonstration

53

demands a new consciousness. A new awareness produces a new situation. This is true of marriage or any other relationship. Marriage provides a new type of experience. Develop the consciousness of being married. It is a new sort of give and take. If two people join in a new union and yet try to remain at the old level, they will soon find themselves out of order. H_2O is more than two parts hydrogen and one part oxygen combined. It is something new, which we call water.

Business partnerships act in the same way to produce something new. Business partners work toward a common goal, yet each must maintain his individualized expression. Each protects his idea or design. Doubts must be kept out. The idea must be kept in order. You are in divine order; your expression is in divine order; your accomplishment is in divine order—because you are the point at which absolute being individualizes itself, and you are its individualization.

Self-Creativeness

Obviously, you did not create yourself, but you do have some part in determining the happenings that occur each day. Infinite Mind individualized itself as you. It then released you with the power of self-locomotion partaking of its wisdom, understanding, and know-how. It gives you power that you can never relinquish. Now what are you going to do with it?

Remember, self-belittlement dishonors your divine relationship. Feelings of inferiority and smallness defame the creative power. The answer is:

1. Complete self-acceptance.
2. Knowing who you are.
3. Projecting this creative power as your creation.

Creative Mind never stops being creative, yet it gives its creation individuality, so you have the right of choice. To progress, this privilege becomes a necessity. Only through your conscious choice can you evolve your spiritual awareness.

The psychologist says, "Believe in yourself." He uses autosuggestion. Science of Mind says, "Know yourself." This is not autosuggestion but the perception of reality. Believe in the self that you really are. You deal with your true nature, which does not change whether you believe in it or ignore it. When you accept yourself, you accept the power of the infinite Mind. If you ignore it, you do not change what you are. Your belief activates your thinking and turns on the power.

Reverse the little doubts and fears as they arise. If you understand the law of being, negative thoughts can be reversed. Moments of discouragement and even despair you also reverse by returning to your spiritual base. The Self which you are cannot be disturbed by reactions. You yourself are the point at which infinite Mind individualizes itself.

Infinite Mind cannot retract its divine announcement. No matter how far you may seem to wander from the divine fiat, you still remain the divine you. Backsliding is only in thought, never in Principle. You never left your divinity; only your thought wandered. This is important to know. You may have periods when your spiritual growth seems to have stopped. It has not. Nothing has happened to you.

Now let's get very positive. Begin to give yourself credit. Rejoice in the divine you. Recognize it as a center of power. You are in conscious control, and you know it. Good things are coming to you because you know they belong to you. That unexpected money came because your consciousness created it. You prosper because your thinking prospers, and you know it. You are well because that is your true nature, and you know it. You merit good friends and happy relationships. Your way is made easy because you give yourself credit for being a creative thinker living harmoniously with the consciousness of good. You know how to make right decisions and stick with them. You are intelligent and mentally alert.

Keep adding to this list, and every time something good comes to you, be quick to give yourself credit. Never mind the negatives; they are not part of you and do not belong to you. They have no effect on you. Give yourself credit for every effort at which you try and succeed. Your demonstration comes because you have created it.

The tree is known by the fruit it bears. In like manner you are known by the demonstrations that you make. The only way you can prove that there is a universal creative power is through creating the experiences that you desire. Infinite Mind fulfills its purpose in you, the conscious creator. This is the divine intent.

Work on the Thing Itself

Do NOT GET caught up in the mechanics of what you are doing. For instance, a student visiting a patient in coronary intensive care concluded that the image was moving across the screen too slowly, so he treated the heart to speed up. Sure enough it did, and the image moved with great speed. He was elated until the nurse rushed in and asked him to leave. He was exciting the patient, she said.

Always treat cause, not effect. Treat for right action; neither *fast* nor *slow* action. Subjective mind will accept that treatment, and the action will be right.

A young actor asked whether he should treat his agent or his manager. Neither. He should treat *himself*. It is his consciousness that gets the work, not the agent. You are the complete law unto whatever you want to do. Establish your consciousness of the right work complete within yourself. Then why have an agent? Because the agent handles the mechanics of the operation. Your demonstration will always bring assistance or supportive action, but the power is in consciousness. This does not mean that you sit at home doing nothing. On the contrary, the greater the power in your affirmative idea, the greater the activity in every area. You may make phone calls or go on interviews, but the demonstration is in your inner conviction. This you establish free from doubt or distrust.

Perhaps you want to sell a house. You sell it in your consciousness. This is a simple, infallible procedure. Consciousness may cause you to put an ad in the paper, call in an agent, or casually drop the word to a friend or even a stranger. Spirit acts through you, but your consciousness of complete action does the work.

Keep the outer activity going, but never lose sight of the Truth. Consciousness does the work. For instance, if you want to sell a car, have your car in excellent condition, clean and

57

shiny—but consciousness produces the customer. You do not pick gold nuggets out of the air, but you do keep all channels of supply open. You anticipate your good coming from all directions. This creates a flexible thought mold, but consciousness establishes your supply. This you know and accept.

You make investments on the action of consciousness. Just as subjective mind establishes heart action, so it establishes right financial action. The power is in consciousness, not in the investment.

You never neglect important details when governed by consciousness. You are at the right place with the right circumstances and conditions. Keep yourself ready and alert, although that alone will not make the demonstration.

When you receive a check for work which you have done, immediately affirm that your consciousness brought it to you. Acknowledge all channels through which your good comes, but recognize that it is your consciousness which brings it to you. When some unexpected pleasure comes, don't grovel in the dust in gratitude, but give thanks that your consciousness brought it to you. Nothing happens by chance; there are no accidents and no miracles. The law of your life acts intelligently and brings to you the thing you want when you make up your mind that you are ready.

Each Idea Has Its Time

THE ONE MIND works by means of ideas you envision. Those ideas are definite, specific, concrete. Each idea has a purpose propelling it. Mind is dynamic knowing. You are its action in form. You can only use those ideas with which you are in rapport. Mind cannot produce something foreign to your nature as your expression. You must feel comfortable in what you do. Your nature results from your conscious choice. The artist, the mechanic, the salesman, as well as those in the healing or legal professions, have all made a conscious choice sometime, someplace.

You learn not to judge by appearances. The tip of the iceberg could be deceiving. You learn to look underneath. Your individual thought is related to a tremendous subjective mind power that goes beyond your perception. You are not what you appear to be, nor is your world what you visibly see. Vision is a subjective force. Look beneath the surface. Understand what your ideas mean. What are your experiences trying to tell you?

Spirit does not preach or tell you what you ought to be and do. Spirit only knows to be. It is not talkative and does not waste time with words. You are its awareness. Begin to see this. You, this minute, are expressing the one Mind. Its specific ideas are the meaningful side of your life.

Vision is inner seeing—who you are—your source at work. Keep centered within. The kingdom is within. God is within. All power is within. Correct your visual habits. Look beyond the appearance. Vision is inner awareness accepted by you.

Alert yourself to your dominant traits. No profession or business is better or less than any other. What is right in your innermost being and gives you the greatest peace is right for you. What inspires you to reach out in those specific inclinations is your best coming through. Your talents talk to you.

You do not have to be a Jack of all trades. The artist may not be business-minded and the financier may find artistic inclinations subsidiary to his main idea. That you cannot pitch a baseball with great accuracy or shoot the ball in the basket should not bring a negative response. When you have enough of any endeavor you can quit. Freedom from a forced expression comes when your vision is clear in the correct perspective.

Look for your tendency to express talents. Stop trying to be what you are not and get the vision of what you are. It's no problem! You don't have to be that which you don't want to be. You are free to choose. Your basic nature is divine. That is something you do not create, but you do choose how you shall express it. Treat for, and meditate on, clear vision; then develop the nature you want to be. There is no mediocrity when you express from the inner vision.

It is your idea that gives you power. Do not try to be what someone wants you to be or what you think you should be. Your ideas must be expressed by you. You are the divine thinker of your own ideas. Stand independent.

You Are All-One

THE POWER IN ANY relationship depends not upon two persons getting along together but in the complete individualization of each. Life unfolds according to personal individualization. We are all part of a universal or cosmic Mind, but each has his or her personal relationship with that Mind. For instance a chorus of 250 voices is very inspiring. Yet it depends on the personal quality and ability of each of those 250 members. Only when this is established does the mighty ensemble take on the aspects of a solid unit. The strength of each augments the strength of the other. It is not what you receive but what you give. This produces strength and joyous reciprocity. Giving, not receiving, is your key.

You develop your own consciousness. No one can do it for you. Consciousness is a personal experience attained by individual effort. You have access to the infinite Mind and to all of it. Your innermost being reveals itself only to you. This awareness you cannot share. Each must have the unique experience himself. You share the *results* of your experience but not the experience. It is a personal participation. No one can eat for you; that will always be personal. No one can sleep for you. You face your God or spiritual awareness alone.

This awareness of the creative Power gives you strength. You feel one with the infinite Mind and one with all the people around you. You are alone with your source yet not lonely. If you reverse this process, loneliness becomes paramount and you smother your identity in your relationship. The greater your aloneness, or all-oneness, the greater your capacity to mingle and be part of your world of expression. Build on your aloneness. Feel its strength and power.

When you wander away from this basic principle, you will become lonely, and you will attempt to compensate by plunging thicker into the crowd. It doesn't work. It throws you further off base. Get back on principle. A trolley car can carry dozens of people as long as it has the contact with power by keeping its trolley on the power line. Within you is the power. Get alone and expand your contact. Loneliness is your signal to get back All-One. Only you can get the power.

This may require much practice on your part. The lonely person may go to a movie or the cocktail lounge. This throws the self further away from its source. Meditate on your oneness with the One. You are one with all the power of the universe, but this must be a daily meditating practice. Get out of the confusion of masses of people who may be off center. Get yourself on center and associate with those who are on center. The quality of your friends reveals to you the quality of your thinking. Attract those with whom you are in rapport. The outside must conform to the inside. The Science of Mind understood and applied means the Science of Mind in your environment and relationships. Stop fooling around. Get back to Principle and stay there.

The people you associate with reveal who you are. Your circle of friends may change as you change. What matters is your all-oneness. Insist that things measure up to that.

Give Until You Enjoy It

GENEROSITY IS ONE of the most important aspects of consciousness. It creates a great reserve of power. Like the automobile, which can easily do 120 miles an hour, it furnishes a reservoir of hidden power that ensures ease and freedom at greater than normal speeds.

Perhaps you should be content when you do all that you have contracted to do. Maybe you put in a full day's work well done. But raises and promotions come because of the extra effort you put in. Generosity does more than you are required to do. It gives more than you have been asked to give. Your awareness of this surplus of power and speed represents growth factors.

On the other hand, look at the grocer who is afraid he might put in an extra coffee bean. He makes sure that he is not going to give more than he is paid for. We brand him as stingy; yet he gives a pound for a pound. This leaves no room for growth or expansion. The law of the tithe states that the first tenth of the harvest goes to the Lord—not one-tenth of just anything you feel like giving after you have first attended to your wants. But the tithe does not work if it is put on a calculation basis. For instance, the person who gives one-tenth provided God gives a fantastic return makes a calculated gesture. The tithe has to be given freely without subconscious bargaining for a return of wealth. It is freely given in love and joy because of our love of God.

The principle of supply, when it is given freely, draws on true generosity. If you give only because you expect to be duly rewarded, you are merely fulfilling the law of demand and supply. This works, but it is a limited concept—a little on the stingy side. When you give because you want to give, you have really grasped the law of supply and have come into a higher law, which we call generosity.

Do what you want to do because you want to do it. That is generosity. To say you will give only to the worthy limits your supply. The tree gives its fruit to any and all. The sun shines and the rain falls on the just and the unjust. The issue is you, not the worthiness or appreciation of the recipient. Generosity concerns your law of prosperity. God SO loved—not just barely, but with a superlative attitude. Don't let the tithe limit what you want to be. How much should you pay or tip? These are deeply related to your law of supply. That extra giving is what makes the difference. That extra bonus. That extra contribution to your church, etc.

Get out of the compulsive. Get away from what is expected of you. Such conditions bring no growth fulfillment. Begin to do what you want to do. Prosperity comes only when you operate from a consciousness of generosity. Can you afford to do what you want to do? Your answer to that question reveals your level of supply. God, or Spirit, does not need your money, nor your affection and praise; yet you need to give to God—money, affection, and praise. But remember, you do not give to get; you give to live. Giving is the measure of your being.

Demonstration Is Definite

YOU ARE CAUSE expressing as effect. As cause in consciousness, you can objectify specific concepts such as money, health, relationships. When there is a lack, subjective mind will attempt to restore the balance. For instance, in the case of overweight, subjective mind will try to compensate. Switching from excessive drinking to excessive smoking does not heal the problem that caused the excess. Oversexiness or greediness represents a lack of balance. The way to compensate is to go back to Principle. Get yourself in spiritual balance. Coordinate by keeping each experience in balance.

Love is not necessarily the fulfillment of every need. It must include your creative thinking. In like manner, your creative thinking must include love. Love and thinking are thus balanced. The introvert detaches himself from life. He develops a one-sided attitude, builds a shell around himself, and lives withdrawn in a subjective world that he alone inhabits. On the other hand, the extrovert lives only in a world of action. He has yet to discover the inner self. Spiritual reality must be explored. The extrovert has to be introduced to the inner world of consciousness. This inside world is the creative world. You cannot have a coin with only one side. You have an inner you and an outer you, but the inner you is the world of creative cause.

You are constantly challenged by the self's four greatest demands—health, wealth, happiness, and love. To sell yourself short in one will produce an abnormal lack in the others. There must be a balance. Don't be too sure you know what your need is. If you did know, you would not be out of balance. Science of Mind practitioners are trained to get you over a problem. In the meantime don't overwork your belief in what you really need. Back off from it and work on the other three. Don't get obsessed over what you think is the trouble. The feeling of financial lack can further the lack. Change your mental direction. You are not that which seems to be. Once you alert yourself to what you have been doing, it is easy to restore your balance. There is no substitute for love. There is no substitute for money, and there is no substitute for health and happiness.

You do not get the money consciousness by sitting in the bank. Consciousness, not the bank, is where your money comes from. You do not get well by working on your physical body. Health is in consciousness, not in the body. Nor do you find love or happiness by having an affair. Love and happiness are found in consciousness. When you establish these attributes within yourself, you experience them in your outer world. The inner and the outer represent the two sides of the coin in perfect balance.

Mind is cause unto every effect. The basic desires exist in consciousness. They are God-ordained and God-ordered. Infinite Mind incorporated these into your being. Your desire for money is the divine concept operating through you. God expects to be rich through you.

Your Financial Flow

You DETERMINE YOUR financial flow. Your money represents your thinking—conscious and subconscious. You are your own paymaster, the *only* paymaster.

Don't be vague regarding your income. Subjective mind works only on specifics. To treat for *money* is not specific enough. Five dollars or five hundred dollars is specific. "Lots of money" could bring you nickels and dimes. You would not accept a position without having some idea as to what it would pay. Even then you might want to negotiate, but you would come to a decision. Two persons doing the same work may be miles apart in what they are paid. It is the consciousness of each one that determines the pay.

People are not paid according to what they are worth but according to their consciousness of specific money. The tip-top executive may get a six-digit salary and yet apparently only work two hours a day. The reverse situation may find a person working around the clock yet getting a mere pittance. You have to get off the money treadmill. Stop working just for money. You will never get anywhere that way. Work for your work; fill your job; put everything into it. Do it well and then go beyond that point. Work is creative action expanding your consciousness. You are not working for money. What *are* you working for? I repeat, you are creative awareness fulfilling its idea of expansion. Everyone should have some form of creative expression. It stimulates the law of growth and destroys the idea of age.

But money is another thing entirely. It could be related, but not necessarily. Money consciousness is apart from work, inheritance, or any channel through which it might come. It is related directly to your specific concept. Money is the action of God manifesting at the level of your understanding. You started with nothing, yet the opportunities quickly manifested at birth. You could only be born into a home that corresponded to the

67

consciousness with which you came. But that changed very quickly, and it will never stop changing. Increase your awareness. Affirm: "I am conscious of abundant supply." But that is not good enough. What is your financial take including salary, interest on investments, etc.? Include everything.

You now have a place to start. Now make your tithe—one tenth to the Lord (law). Do not try to use gargantuan figures. It won't mean anything to you. Nor can you get anywhere by affirming that all that the Father hath belongs to you. That is true in theory, but in practice only your consciousness of *specific* money determines what you shall get. Why not start with ten percent? Make your treatment, "I have the consciousness of *x* dollars a week." Demonstrate that. Now give yourself another "raise." Maybe you do not need to work in ten-percent ranges. Many certainly should not. Many can double their income. It is up to you. Whatever amount you set requires that you treat each day on its consummation.

Remember, it is your consciousness you are working on. God knows only abundance, but that does not do the work for you. You establish the level at which your finances unfold. Are you a stingy paymaster—or do you rejoice in seeing people prosper? You are rich with infinite substance. Your thought is the spearhead for its continuous flow. Your money flow never dries up.

The Consciousness
of Nowness

How long does it take to make a demonstration? There is no time element involved. It is all consciousness, and consciousness knows only the now. Your demonstration is never made in time but in consciousness. It is a *now* experience. How long is *now*? It is where you are and is what you are. Get the conviction of who you are *now*. Your acceptance is the cue.

How close are you to your demonstration? That question would imply space and distance. All the qualities and the substance of your demonstration are within you. Your thinking about your specific desires activates their equivalent within you. This is the way it works: Each idea which you accept with conviction as the truth of your being releases its counterpart in consciousness. Each idea becomes a here-and-now experience. Spirit is complete within you here and now.

You are awakening and unfolding divine attributes that are part of the real you. During sleep you do not cease to be, although it might appear that way. Your memories do not disappear, and when you arise in the morning, you summon all your attributes to keep going. The immortal you has all its attributes fully established within you. Only you can awaken them, and it must be a now and here event. Your thought of a future brings no response because Spirit is a now experience. You are a now God-awareness. This has been the basis of the I AM concept even since before Moses announced it.

Consciousness has no past and no future. Affirmations of Truth may be your method of self-acceptance. Try it. Your affirmation is directed at the invisible you. It turns away from any appearance and focuses its thought at the point of creativity. You are one with the cosmic Mind; therefore you can accept this reality. Only that of which you are aware exists for you. This means that whatever you experience is within you. You are not in Chicago or Los Angeles until you are aware that Chicago and Los Angeles exist within you. All places and experiences could be the same, but your consciousness designates what they shall be. You are not in your work. Your work is in you. Your office, your factory, the place where you live are all in you. You don't live in your body; your body lives in you. Everything that you experience is in you.

Your outer expression is the projection of your inner awareness. You can change the outside very quickly by changing your inner awareness. The creative power endowed you with the ability to make your world what you want it to be. This action takes place in consciousness. Your limitless success consciousness can be experienced. Its unfoldment depends on your acceptance.

When will your prayer be answered? The only thing between you and your demonstration is dormant thinking. Now is the time and here is the place. You don't have to wait; much healing is instantaneous. All that you seek is within. Treat that you are free from belief in time and space. Demonstration is clear thinking about the idea you want to express. Change your belief from not having to that of having, recognizing that the creative consciousness accepts what you think with conviction. Demonstrations are instantaneous as you accept your idea as already being right here and right now. This is the day of salvation, and now is the moment of acceptance.

Realization

REALIZATION IS THE HIGHEST form of treatment and the goal toward which we all strive. But it is first necessary to understand fully the techniques involved in affirmations and denials. You are not making a compromise. You learn to walk before you run. In like manner, you understand your relationship to your world. You are not body; you are Spirit. this may not be an instantaneous realization. You grow in consciousness and attain true spiritual realization. In your mind you separate body and consciousness, environment and awareness, the outer and the inner. The self of you is not physical; it is spiritual. It is consciousness. You move in a material world but are not of it. Do not negate the material world. It is thought reflected and manifested, but it is not you.

This realization is necessary for you to go forward, for your thought must be untouched by the surrounding world. You establish yourself at the God level. You identify, not with your world of form, but with attributes of Spirit. Instead of identifying with money, you identify with that which creates money. You concentrate on being instead of doing. You are that which is complete. At this point, nothing you do can add to that completeness. You depend on divine Principle because you are divine Principle. You will be conscious, at this level, of that which creates all that there is in your individualized world.

This method of self-realization releases the true being which the self is. You become that perfection in which there is no sickness. This spiritual awareness can be translated into terms of your life-expression. What you know yourself to be, you begin to consciously express. Since you are one with God, or perfect Spirit, you let that perfect Being express. The positive, divine attributes of which you become aware are a tremendous spiritual force pushing through you to find expression.

71

Whatever you desire to express in your outer world must first be realized as existing within your consciousness. This is the creative awareness portrayed in the book of Genesis. The illumined Consciousness said, "Let there be light," and there was light. That same Consciousness said, "Let the perfect self appear," and man emerged as its own image and likeness.

You redeem, or rename, your material world. You let whatever you want to experience appear. You identify with creative Substance and speak your idea or word into it. No struggle, no resistance—the idea is propelled by infinite Mind.

The healing is in your consciousness. The work is done within you, as you. Heaven is your state of consciousness, and earth is whatever you have chosen to manifest. It is as simple as that. No force is working against you, and you do not have to combat someone's negative belief. You are the complete Law, God becoming aware of God through you and expressing through your actions. All the power of God is focused on your being. You realize one Mind and one manifest world—all good.

Life Is Principle

THIS, THE CLOSING essay of the Basic Principles series, takes you right back to the place where you started. Nothing ever closes, for your perception reveals steps you had not envisioned. No matter how far you go or how advanced you may feel you are, your basic principle is God, the Good, expressing as Mind through your thought. The important thing is that you never lose the consciousness of the original life impulse. What infinite Mind thought you to be has never ceased to be the driving force in your life and has never diminished in its power. So the end and the beginning are identical, for each is Spirit at its highest level of understanding.

Once you establish this conviction of the infinite power of consciousness, you will find that it influences everything you do. You keep in this awareness that the original consciousness is the only power and that it is working in each thing that you are doing. You never let your consciousness drop to the level of the outer experience. You stay centered in the One, and the experience is brought up to where you are. You don't drop to the level of the outside thing. The outside thing must be transcended and lifted to the point of consciousness where you are.

Always, you are the center of creativity, and all objective experiences, no matter what they may appear to be, have to be brought into relation with your inner awareness. If an experience cannot stand that test, then the experience does not belong to you. If the experience cannot be brought into the light of Truth, it will destroy itself once your support is withdrawn from it.

Error and confusion cannot exist in your world unless you support them. This is why people who spend so much time thinking about what they want to get rid of find that the negation becomes fastened to them. What you think about, you endow with the presence of yourself. What you think about becomes a part of your experience. You should never go places where you do not want to be seen or do things you don't want to be identified with. Your attendance becomes your endorsement unless you make a recognizable protest.

For the Science of Mind student, life is not a school but an opportunity to express what you really are. At this level, you create your own experiences. Your expression reflects the truth of your being. No matter what you are doing, you know the originating power is the power in your actions. You stand on Principle. Your whole demonstration is Principle. *Life is Principle.* This is always fulfilled.

Your Purpose

The Power of Purpose

SUCCESSFUL PEOPLE ARE motivated by purpose, and all of their activities are geared toward achieving that goal. The purpose must be one in which you can put all of your creativeness. Your interest must be all-consuming. Lacking a powerful, positive purpose, an individual's life has no direction. Lethargy and inertia are bound to settle in.

Fortified with a purpose you can never settle for half-way measures. You know where you are going and why. What you do is important to you, because life is important. This purpose gives direction to all activities. This does not necessarily mean that you are single-minded. Although extreme specialization seems to be the rule with physicians, lawyers, and business consultants, in other areas exactly the opposite is the case.

For instance, President Dwight Eisenhower, a multi-talented individual, was an outstanding military figure, statesman, and painter. Similarly, Winston Churchill was a great naval officer, statesman, painter, and author. Many famous athletes, actors, and writers have become musicians of note. But whatever the purpose, whether it seems great or small, the intensity of your creativeness and enthusiasm gives it its power. It must have tremendous meaning to you, and you must have great anticipation of its complete fulfillment.

Believe in your divine calling. "Even for this same purpose have I raised thee up, that I might show my power in you." While you may have many problems and face almost insurmountable difficulties, your power is in your purpose. You must know where you are going and why, and you depend on a guiding Intelligence to get you there.

It is much easier to work successfully when you relate your purpose to life. The athlete may not particularly enjoy strenuous exercise and discipline, but he or she relates it to the strength and power necessary for attainment. Without purpose,

77

you scatter energy. Purpose conserves and directs. The purpose in treatment is not merely to control your thinking but to develop the power of creative thought so that you can produce in your experience the conditions you desire. The sincerity of your purpose controls everything that you do. You *can* attain your objective.

Planning Your Purpose

WHILE YOUR ACTIONS are motivated by your purpose, careful planning is necessary for its fulfillment. For instance, when your purpose to build a house becomes powerful, you begin to plan it. This is where the architect would come in. His blueprint is simply his thought expressed on paper. He outpictures what is in his mind. The modern interior designer would have a scale model of each room with a scale model of each piece of furniture that is to go into a room. Perhaps he would try many different arrangements before he settled upon the one he thought would be the best.

Success in any field of activity does not happen; it is planned. The homemaker plans the dinner, the businessman plans his day. One of the founders of the Million Dollar Club, which is composed of people who write over a million dollars' worth of insurance each year, as soon as he arrives in his office writes on his desk calendar the dollar value of the policies which he will write that day. His mental plan works. His purpose is to make money, and his plan is to sell insurance. He believes that his business proposition is good for his client, and he adjusts the plan to his client's need.

A person who wants to be a singer or accountant or lawyer must plan a systematic method of study that will confer the ability to be that which he or she wants to be. A person who wants to take a good vacation must plan what she is going to do and how she is going to do it. You are motivated by what you believe is your purpose in life. Whether your purpose is to be a mother, an attorney, a business executive, or a teacher, you must have a plan for fulfilling that purpose. Perhaps your purpose is to be a complete self—the divine being that God intended you to be. Then plan how this purpose is going to be attained.

You cannot develop your real power if you are irresponsible. Planned responsibility is necessary to fulfill your purpose. Don't be afraid to make plans and to change them as your mental capacity increases. Do not become a slave to your plan. You made it, and only you can change it. Make your plan work for you and not you for it. It will respond.

Organizing Your Purpose

To ORGANIZE MEANS to arrange or constitute into a coherent unity in which each part has a special function or relationship. Obviously, the successful person is one who operates in this way. So does a business corporation; all departments must work together. This same rule applies to you and your purpose. Your life purpose is inescapable. Its scope provides a frame of reference to which all the experiences you will ever have will be related. You can change your experiences only when you change your purpose, consciously or unconsciously. Everything you do is related to this purpose.

Since Mind is infinite, the more ideas it reveals to you, the greater your need to coordinate them. Different thoughts and feelings must be brought together into their right relationship. Bring all ideas into alignment with your purpose. Don't go off on a tangent or let impatience undermine this purpose.

Eagerly accept ideas that fit into your purpose, for your purpose will be a constantly expanding mental experience. You constantly draw to yourself greater opportunities.

Modern business spends millions of dollars each year on research to find how to better its products. Get as many different concepts as you possibly can on fulfilling your purpose, but organize them; bring them together and make them work for you.

In your mental treatments, watch the ideas which work for you. See how they are constantly branching off, yet maintaining a relationship to the purpose of your treatment. Expand your thinking about each thing that you do. Mind is infinite, but organize the ideas as they unfold so that you keep them definitely related. Feeling sorry for yourself is servile activity; so is thinking in terms of lack or limitation.

Turn away from these disruptive thoughts by cultivating self-acceptance, self-respect. Realize that you are appreciated and that you are appreciative of others. Think definitely in terms of prosperous, abundant living. Plan a complete new train of ideas; then keep them organized and unified.

Carrying Out Your Purpose

THE PROOF OF WHAT you believe is revealed by how you act. You cannot delay the fulfillment of your purpose when you plan it and organize all ideas related to it. You should not put off what you want to do but should put your ideas to work for you. The thought becomes the thing. The word becomes flesh. What you think, you express.

You carry out your own orders; therefore you are the only authority. The successful executive can delegate his or her work to others. There is a universal, creative Mind that is subject to your thought, but it cannot do anything for you unless you tell it what to do. You must act with certainty. There is no one anywhere that can oppose you but yourself. Consequently, there is no need to approach any situation with fear and trembling.

Act with authority. The whole world respects the person that can act with authority. Your authority is over yourself. You do not carry out your orders by willpower. Never try to force a situation or to coerce a person. Authority is your inner knowingness, your conviction of Truth. You command yourself. The prophets of ancient times always spoke with authority—"Thus saith the Lord." You are this same authority. Within you the one Mind reveals to you what you need to know about yourself and what you need to do. Speak your word, then, with power; you *are* in command of every situation.

Great men and women are always filled with the conviction of purpose which cannot be stopped. The mind that reveals to you the purpose is the same power that will work through you toward its fulfillment. Ideas which come to you come to be expressed and fulfilled. The purpose of the seed is to become a plant that produces flowers and fruit. Its action is a pushing out from an invisible power at its center. In like manner, your purpose contains an invisible power that works inevitably to its fulfillment. Don't stop until you have accomplished your purpose.

83

This is the right way for its fulfillment. The Infinite cannot be frustrated, and the divine purpose of your life works ceaselessly to accomplish its fulfillment.

Principles at Work

Good-Conscious

GOD, THE GOOD, is the basic power that you express. This divine Mind is everywhere present. Each of us is this Mind, or Good, individualized. We need to become Good-conscious and Good-oriented. When things are not expressing in the right manner, your mind gets focused on all the things that seem to be wrong. You have to stop thinking of the wrongness of conditions, for as long as you do so, you energize it as the wrong experience.

You should never run away from any experience, but instead understand the creative process. What you think about objectifies as your experience. Every experience you have represents something of your belief and thinking. Something within your consciousness energized it, or it could not have been. To change a situation, you must reverse the direction of your energy. Instead of thinking toward the outward expression, you must focus your energy on a new concept, the way in which you want things to appear. Instead of wrong finances, think of right finances. Instead of being stymied and in a rut, think of right activity adequately expressing. There is a principle of God in you, and you should think in terms of this good.

The power to do good is greater than any inclination to do wrong. The power to build up is a greater force than the power to tear down. All of your actions take the direction of your dominant thinking. If you feel inadequate, you will make yourself act inadequately. You may have the ability to be very efficient, but your actions have to conform to your dominant belief. Your belief that you are inadequate will keep you from putting your best effort into what you do.

On the other hand, belief in Good becomes an acceptance of your true creative power and your real purpose. You think Good because that is the way in which you were conceived. You think

Good because you are endowed with the power to maintain Good. When God, or infinite Mind, proclaimed its creation as very good, humanity received all the power necessary to be very good. Every negative impression should always be reversed in your realization of the allness and completeness of Good. The consciousness of Good demonstrates the Science of Mind.

Every Moment Is Important

YOU CANNOT DIVIDE your time into periods of varying importance. Every moment is essential to your well-being. Since all you will ever know is in the immediate now, the moment of which you are aware becomes the most important one to you. You may appraise your experiences in such a way that some things do seem of greater value than others, and this may well be so. But regardless of what you are doing, the moment of doing it contains the essence of all you shall ever be. This moment affords you your creative opportunity.

What you think in this moment determines whether you will create unpleasantness or success. You can strike out boldly, emancipating yourself from the bondage of past recollections, good or bad, and create in this moment the quality of experiences that really belongs to you. You were born to unfold the divine pattern, just as the seed unfolds the tree. The progressive individual never gives in to difficulties but instead rises above them so quickly that they cannot impress themselves upon his or her subconscious. Conscious creativeness is the law of personal growth and unfoldment.

Since you create your experiences, you learn to perceive all that is involved within their creative cause. That which is in your consciousness at the present moment determines what will appear. Every individual is a prophet and can prophesy correctly the type of experience he or she is going to have. Since you are a thinking, creating individual, the power in this moment is determined by the thinking in this moment. You can shut out confusion and establish harmony.

The ability to change your mind is your greatest asset. When you have had enough of anything, you can quit. When you perceive the consequences of negative thinking, you can change to creative, constructive ideas. When a dog attacks a porcupine and has to be taken to surgery to have the quills extracted, it seldom attacks a porcupine again.

89

The intelligence in you enables you to see the direction of your thinking and where such trends are taking you. The only thing that can change your direction is a change of mind. This moment you have complete power to accept your conscious creativeness. All of your infinite possibilities exist right here in the now.

The Power of Treatment

THROUGH TREATMENT YOU cause a mental law of creativeness to produce what it would not do otherwise. In the same way, the bulb that you place in the ground causes the soil to do things it would not do otherwise. Whether it produces lilies, tulips, or gladioli depends on what you have given it to do. Creative Mind also responds according to what you give it to do.

Treatment is a step-by-step process. While there is no limit to what you can demonstrate, you should give full attention to each idea one at a time. A treatment for prosperity should not be interspersed with thoughts of love or health. The treatment should make you aware of the source and substance of your supply. You keep in the consciousness of this abundant supply. It should move step by step toward the elimination of all belief in lack or limitation. It should erase each specific concept of lack. From the elimination of lack, the treatment develops the awareness of abundance. It brings forth your prosperous being.

Undesirable appearances have to be removed just as a forty-story skyscraper that has become outmoded is torn down before the ninety-story high-rise can be built. Treatment clears the mind of false beliefs.

The length of time you spend on a treatment depends on how soon you arrive at an inner conviction that the work is accomplished. As soon as this occurs, you rest your thought in peace, knowing that perfect right action has already taken over.

Then you are ready to treat for something else. Make each phase of your treatment deliberate and definite. You are working to create belief and acceptance in your mind. Definiteness is the keynote of demonstration. Universal subjective mind does not care what it is objectifying for you. It knows only to do. Its nature is to fulfill. But when you are hesitant for fear of asking too much, you are personally limiting yourself. When you make a demand upon yourself through creative Mind, you rise and meet the demand.

The Great Miracle

No MATTER WHAT your past experiences have been, new hope and new vision will inevitably change your life. Out of darkness comes light. This is the principle of resurrection. Each morning upon arising you make a fresh start. There is no reason for any person to think him- or herself defeated or frustrated. The new day holds new possibilities. The *life* urge is greater than any negative appearance or obstruction.

You are greater than anything you do or any work in which you might be engaged. If opposition seems to be too great, you must clarify your vision of what you are trying to do and your ability to do it. The athlete carefully measures the height of the hurdle with his or her eye and then proceeds to clear it. A ship is built to withstand the stresses to which it will be exposed. A bridge is built to carry the load that will go over it. Your mind is built to think creatively. There is nothing miraculous about this; it is a natural law.

You need to measure your mental, spiritual capacity. You need to know how much spiritual energy you must expend to meet any demand upon you. Statistics show that 85 percent of the people who lose their positions do so not because of inability to do their work but because of personality problems. You need to look at your personality with the same mental eye as the athlete measuring the hurdle. When you recognize at what point your patience or tolerance breaks down, you can do something about it. Peace, poise, and consideration of others are attributes that you can develop to get over the emotional hurdle.

Man is infinite intelligence, and you can improve your use of this intelligence to bring forth success in your life. This change of thought is what the resurrection signifies. You mentally rise above the discouragement and narrow thinking. God, infinite Good, knows no limit, and you can function at this God level. Every day you commence to live.

On Freedom

FREEDOM IS NOT merely an escape from oppression and bondage but is a creative action moving into a larger sphere of life itself. Many people never seem to get beyond the stage of asserting the kinds of experiences they do not want. They think only of what they have had enough of. The negative aspect may be a strong incentive in growth, for when your environment cramps and restricts you, you can move out of it. But the important thing is what you are moving into. What you came from is not as significant as what you are being and becoming. Whether childhood was painful or pleasant is not too essential. Whichever experience you had is left behind when you move into adulthood, for your vision and incentive will open up new experiences for you.

When you go forward to a new awareness of unfolding life, you are not in bondage to the past experience in your own mind. You are creative by nature—physically, emotionally, and spiritually. Perhaps we cannot divide these areas. As civilization progresses, the creative level rises. You learn that the bondage is in your mind and so is the freedom.

But you cannot find freedom without ideas. It is your creative thought that establishes the new expression for you. There is no limit to what you can create once you recognize the power of your own mind. Although we readily assume that we were endowed with the right to be free, we have not recognized that there is a way in which this freedom works. It is not an automatic process. We take many of our difficult experiences hard. Tolerance, or suffering it to be so, seems to be as far as we can go. Spiritual growth is not mechanical, nor is it accomplished through suffering or as the result of pain.

The steps in the creative process are all forward projects. Spirit is that which knows no resistance. "Let there be light. Let us make man in our own image and likeness." These are forward projects based on new concepts and new experiences. Don't look at your escape from the past as freedom. Get a new idea, new vision, and freedom in the joy of expressing your creativeness.

Power-Producing Conditions

ORISON SWETT MARDEN, one of the pioneer New Thought thinkers, wrote: "Holding the poverty thought keeps one in touch with poverty-producing conditions."

Your thinking always supports itself. The person who feels inferior is constantly supporting the inferiority belief by giving reasons for it. Each idea supports itself to sustain or explain its expression. This is true of either the positive or the negative concept. Your awareness of good keeps you unified with good-producing conditions. The law of right action creates support for right thinking.

People may not change their beliefs easily or quickly. Deep-seated beliefs have established a train of activity in which unconsciously the individual is constantly reinforcing his or her belief. No one abandons a belief until convinced of the importance of a new belief. Emerson said:

> The key to every man is his thought. Sturdy and defying though he look, he has a helm which he obeys, which is the idea after which all his facts are classified. He can only be reformed by showing him a new idea which commands his own.

You cannot dislodge old ideas until you are convinced of something better. For instance, ask most people with a problem why they are not succeeding. They will give you many reasons why. Unconsciously they have entrenched themselves in believing in causes that produce lack of success. Or they will say that they would like to get out of a negative situation but will proceed to argue as to why they cannot. Subconsciously they have kept in touch with limitation-producing conditions. The law of Mind knows no limitations, because it always operates effortlessly at the level of your thought. It is free to be whatever you think yourself to be. Mind is infinite and you have limitless possibilities.

Clear vision always brings with it thoughts necessary to reinforce it and to guarantee its fulfillment. A bridge is only as strong as its supports. Your vision, in like manner, depends upon the support that your conviction and desire give it. Whatever thought you sustain and accept as your belief—health, wealth, or love—keeps you in touch with health-, wealth-, or love-producing conditions. That is the way life produces.

Goodwill

THE AGE-OLD promise of "peace on earth to men of good will" clearly emphasizes the law of consciousness. Whatever good you want to experience you must first make a reality within your own thinking and feeling. An erratic disposition is not at peace. The Science of Mind shows how you can get control of your moods. For centuries people have tried to establish peace without realizing the necessity of removing their inner conflicts. Since consciousness is the cause, and your relationships are the effect, you must come to a sense of peace within yourself. Humanity at one with God is humanity at peace with itself.

When humanity separates itself from its Source its expression becomes dualistic: humanity and God, good and evil. This attitude spreads itself so that conditions in your world seem to have an opposing or evil power like a Frankenstein's monster, which you in turn fear and fight. You need only realize that you created the thing that you are fighting, and in like manner your thought can uncreate it. The creator is always greater than his or her creation, and you are greater than the environment you create.

Turning in thought from experiences on the outside to the creative Source within restores your soul. It produces goodwill and peace. This goodwill refrains from judging other people. It knows that each person is in his or her right place doing what is right for him or her at that time. It means friendliness, considerateness, and kindness. People of goodwill find peace.

Agendas for Living

EVERY ORGANIZATION THAT follows parliamentary law has an agenda for each meeting, which programs the business to be presented and the order in which the discussions shall follow. Your personal agenda, which you should have, must follow the same procedure. Your plans are important. Your objectives give incentive to your life. The greater your interest and enthusiasm, the greater momentum your business and affairs will have.

As important as the objective may be, the order in which it is to be unfolded is equally important. The creative sequence cannot be disrupted. The thought precedes the thing. In consciousness you find the cause for whatever you are going to do, and every cause has its own effect. Health and wealth are both effects rather than causes. Success is a state of mind in which you find the creative cause of prosperity. You are prosperous when you are success-conscious. This is the right creative sequence. In like manner, not only will you be happy because things are going right, but you will find that things go right because of your inner happiness.

The principle of supply is limitless, but in your experience it will take the form that your consciousness gives it. You should become success-conscious, health-conscious, and money-conscious.

This same order must be observed in your health agenda. The great psychologist William James called New Thought "the religion of healthy-mindedness." Your attitude must be free from frustration and negative beliefs. Your positive thinking must be constructive. Creative Spirit endowed you with the ability to be well.

The most important item on each person's agenda is to attain his or her complete individuality. You should develop an inner poise and confidence that nothing can disturb. This can be

98

done only through recognizing your oneness with the creative Spirit itself. You are part of a universal wholeness. In this strength lies your freedom. The God-ordained self of each of us is destined to become fully conscious of its dominion. Then it can speak with authority.

What about Your Contract?

EVERY SUCCESSFUL PERSON has a secret agreement with him- or herself, or a covenant with God. It may not be clearly defined mentally but may be more an inner feeling. Nevertheless, it becomes a contract.

You should recognize this secret goal, whatever it might be. No matter how remote the possibilities of its attainment might seem, you should bring it into its true perspective. If it still seems unattainable, perhaps it is not the real goal. In that event you should go deeper into your consciousness and find another goal.

Henry Ford was over forty before he got started successfully. His main goal was to develop mass production in order to make cheaper transportation available to every family. Wealth was not his objective, but through fulfilling his real pattern, wealth came also. Everything he touched prospered.

Metropolitan Opera baritone Lawrence Tibbett's great love was to sing; that was his concept of success. When he suddenly realized that he was being handsomely paid for what he loved to do, it seemed a miracle. He was doing what he really wanted to do, and getting money for it.

There is nothing wrong in your motive to make money, and such an urge would have to be fulfilled. However, something within the self has made a secret covenant to attain additional goals.

You would make a great mistake if you limited your expression to the attainment of just one goal. To have health and wealth but not love would make life very incomplete. If you go deep enough into consciousness you will discover your secret agreement to bring forth your God-intended self in all its power, complete and whole. You must have faith in your contract.

Henry Ford said:

I believe that faith works. If a man starts doing something he believes in, and does it with a motive which the universe can respect—that is, to make life more livable for others as well as for himself—his belief in this work will draw to him the means to do the work.

One-Pointed Demonstration

WHILE ALL OF US undoubtedly work on many different things at the same time, we must make sure that we do not scatter our energy. No matter how many different ideas you might be working on, you should keep them all tied together—just as a merchant may sell many different products but would not tend to overemphasize one particular item and neglect the others. The overall pattern for the merchant would be that all merchandise move profitably. A broker may sell many different lines of stock, but his emphasis would be on his consciousness of successful selling. A spiritual mind practitioner, during the course of a week, would handle many cases. Each one would merit his or her full attention, yet the point of emphasis is on the practitioner's healing.

Individually, each person may be working on many different points of self-improvement. This might include mental discipline, emotional equilibrium, good physical grooming, correct posture, and a well-rounded personality. But the point of emphasis would be the consciousness of a completely integrated self in complete control of everything in its life.

In using the Science of Mind, you should have a list on which you are treating. Every item would be covered every day, but the overall pattern would be the spiritual self asserting its dominion. This one-pointedness is essential to demonstration, otherwise your mental energy will be scattered or you might be caught up in varying emotional states. Through one-pointed thinking, your emotions can never betray you or deceive you. You can use your emotions to express what you are and not let your emotions tell you how you shall feel.

Your successful self can govern on every plane of experience. Your awareness of what you really are can command everything that comes into your life. God, or divine Mind, is the source and substance of all life. One-pointedness sees only the perfect source and maintains the perfect outlet.

The Law of Consciousness

CONDITIONS IN YOUR life correspond to ideas and convictions within your consciousness. You should not be disturbed by any experience that does not measure up to your standard, because you have the power to change the experience. Since experiences reflect states of mind, the creative cause should concern you far more than its effect. A new mental cause will change the material manifestation.

True, there is a higher consciousness than our ordinary concept of cause and effect, which seems concerned only with our daily activities. This higher consciousness is First Cause, God, or your origin of being. There is but one Mind: God, infinite Good. This Mind is the source of that which you are. Consequently, you live, move, and have your being as perfect idea in this infinite Mind. Through your understanding of mental causation you learn how infinite Mind operates through you in your affairs. Each individual can thus keep him- or herself unified with this great creative power of the universe or through careless negative thinking can shut off this power.

The purpose of life is to recognize the true source and nature of the self and its power. You can learn to let your true nature assert itself. In this higher awareness there is only good, and it can bring only good to you. The infinite Mind includes us in its well-being. If you do not interefere by blocking this life stream with your negative thought, it will always express its complete right action in everything that concerns you.

This higher consciousness links you with universal Mind and maintains its universal awareness. Instead of thinking from limited concepts, you function in a higher consciousness where all is established as right. You perceive your perfection not as the creation of your own thought but as a divine reality that transcends personal thinking.

This higher consciousness is all-wise and yet all love. It is completeness of being. You unify with this higher consciousness not in order to change your world but because it is perfection and the way life really is. Thus you become aware of your conscious oneness with all life and truth. This consciousness expresses as a new world for you.

Make Up Your Mind

EACH NEW DAY challenges you to make new plans. A periodic checkup on thoughts and desires is very valuable.

The greater your spiritual growth and unfoldment, the more essential becomes an intelligent plan. We would have weird architecture and buildings if the builders refused to follow a blueprint because they felt it would restrict them. Without a plan, they would end up with architectural monstrosities.

A modern architect whom you would engage to build a home for you would plan very carefully. He or she would want to know what kind of house you wanted: the size, style, and decor. Your architect would go into great detail trying to meet your requirements and give you what you wanted. But more than that, he or she would want to get acquainted with you and would want to know what kind of people were going to live here, what you really liked and did not like. This new home must reflect you. It would be your personality in a living expression. Your consciousness would flow through the fixed forms and designs that your architect executed.

Of course this is only common sense, for all of your life-expression must be the movement of your consciousness. Your career, the classes you attend, your reading, and your recreation are simply the flowing of your own consciousness. So you do make plans. You even set milestones or schedules just as when traveling you would decide in which city you would spend the night.

Make up your mind. You do not accomplish very much until you decide what you really want to accomplish. When you have made up your mind with conviction, that is all there is to it. There is no use of willpower or coercion. Make up your mind, and be what you want to be.

Principles Applied

The Source of Your Energy

TREATMENT IS NOT trying to make yourself believe something that is not so, but it is based upon truth. It is to change your belief so that you can recognize and accept the truth.

The truth is that you are the expression of infinite Mind, that within is all of the potential of God—all of the creative energy of the universe. This is the truth. When you reach outside of yourself for that which is within you, it is very obvious that you do not believe that it is within you. Therefore, your treatment must change your belief so that you stop this almost ceaseless looking for things beyond or outside the self and recognize that with the *self* there is all wisdom, all intelligence, all power, and all life.

Your treatment is the affirmation of this truth. Treatment works not upon the infinite Mind, because the Infinite has already operated and established its work. Your treatment operates upon you. It breaks down the resistances within you and eliminates false concepts. It wipes out of your consciousness the belief in obstruction. It restores you to the recognition that you are in the stream of life, and the stream of life is constantly expressing as you.

You must realize that the infinite energy of the universe is within you, and in this consciousness of the one Mind, there is no energy crisis, because energy is infinite Mind. You look not to channels nor to physical sources. You look to the real source, the originating life power. This infinite Mind is the energy of life. Infinite Mind cannot be depleted in energy, so there is nothing in you that can believe in depletion or lack of energy. Your consciousness of infinite energy can bring complete renewal in your thought. The supremacy of Spirit, the creativeness of God, the omnipresence of Good—these concepts are the source of your energy, and these are the truths that you affirm for yourself, for your country, for your world.

All false belief is wiped out so that you have the conviction of infinite, limitless possibilities. You *know* that the one Mind, in all of its infiniteness of being, right now is all vitality. You put a premium on your spiritual-mental energy, so right now you value your thought. You choose what you shall think with great deliberation and care. You do not scatter your mental energy by trivial thinking. You put a value upon your time so that you do not waste time, for there is nothing anywhere in life except the energy of Mind. You are that Mind energized in perfect action doing its perfect work, knowing its perfection of being.

In this consciousness of the one Source and the one Supply, there is no panic-ness anywhere, because the one Mind, in its infinite being, does its perfect work and reveals that which it *is*—infinite energy, infinite Mind, inexhaustible strength, limitless power. This is the truth of being, and *this* you accept.

You Are Not the Experience

KEEP YOURSELF DETACHED from the conditions around you. This is important. The Self is never part of the experiences which you may have. It is your absolute being. God manifesting as you. Mind knowing itself as you. All cause originates here. Conditions are reflections of states of mind and have no cause of their own. They are effects of mental action. They have no authority over you. Their only power rests in what you believe about them. Since cause is in mind, detachment is necessary for the full power to manifest in the cause.

This does not mean that the experiences do not exist. They do. Like the garment you wear—you put it on or take it off. The power is in your consciousness, not in the garment. The Science of Mind shows that the power is in your mind—that you think of yourself as Mind creating. This causes things to happen on the outside. You apply the full creative power at the creative point—the mind. Thus you act not as a physical being but as mind. Your consciousness is centered here, not in physical awareness.

As your belief accepts this truth, you are in a position to take charge of your life.

When you want to change a condition or heal an appearance, detach yourself from it. Do not deny that it exists—detach yourself from it. Look at it: it is not you any more than the suit is you—or than the sickness is—or than the financial limitation is.

It is not you, but there is a relationship between the experience and you. If you believe you are the experience, you have no basis for changing it. You are not the experience. You are *having* an experience.

Keep Faith with Yourself

BELIEVE IN YOUR ability and recognize your developed talents. There is a right place for your ability to express and for your talents to be appreciated. Keep faith with yourself, because until you keep faith with yourself, you cannot keep faith with people, and people will not keep faith with you.

It is easy to recognize the individual who has faith in him- or herself. This person is not overconfident or arrogant, and not humble either. There is a sense of assurance, a postiveness that is not overbearing, a demeanor that inspires you. You recognize that such a person knows who he or she is, knows what's going on, and knows how to attain goals.

Build up faith in yourself by believing in your true ability; believing in your capacity to grow; believing that you have a mission. You have something to do. You have something worthwhile to accomplish. You are just as necessary to the Infinite as the Infinite is necessary to you. But you must know all of this and keep faith with these ideas. When you know there is purpose in what you do, you can never feel let down. Don't break faith with yourself. Believe in your power, and even when you do not consciously see how things are going to work out, keep faith with yourself.

> I do not ask to see the distant scene;
> One step enough for me.

It is this one step that establishes your faith, and it is taking one step at a time that shows you keep faith with yourself.

No matter how many people may doubt you, don't doubt yourself. No matter how many people may seem discouraged or try to discourage you, don't break faith with yourself. Infinite Mind reveals to you the rightness of your place, and at the center of your being this infinite Mind whispers your name. You are its image and likeness; you are its infinite expression. Infinite Mind reveals to you that which you are. Keep faith with yourself and the world will keep faith with you.

Support Your Belief

EACH PERSON'S BELIEF is the law of his or her expression. It establishes the pattern through which all of a person's experiences appear. You have many subjective beliefs that operate below your threshold of conscious awareness. They will continue to function unless you do something to alter them, or until their intensity diminishes to such a point that no power is left in them.

This stresses the importance of knowing what you believe and why you believe it. You thus recognize the beliefs that you want to continue and know how to eliminate those that no longer serve you. The beliefs that you choose to continue governing you must be reinforced by you. What you believe and want to happen must be supported by your thinking and your feelings. You need to spend more time thinking about your dominant beliefs and how you can actually strengthen them.

This is what treatment work does, and this is why you emphasize that whatever you want to demonstrate, you should treat adequately until the manifestation is complete. This steadfastness of treatment is necessary especially where people are susceptible to change. Many people are fickle in their beliefs. They are torn between the power of creative consciousness and their belief that environment has power over them. They claim that the cause is in Mind and yet act as though the effect is the cause. This is why your belief must be supported. Mind is the creative power; therefore you must believe this and let your actions support your belief.

One of the classic illustrations of this is the children of Israel praying for rain and Elijah telling them to dig ditches to receive it. Many of the crowd ridiculed him because there had been a drought for years, with no sign of a cloud in the sky. But Elijah recognized that the belief must be supported by action in order to be an operative one.

Your actions must prove that you expect your treatment to work. Therefore you must make preparation for that which you are working to receive. The person treating for a new career should prepare himself for that career. This means acquiring skills and abilities necessary for the new venture. Always watch your belief and make all of your thinking support that belief. For the belief has to express at the level of your awareness.

Reinforcements

YOUR VISION OPERATES like an advance guard. It precedes every demonstration. It should be clear—actually embodying, in its mental perception, what you really want to accomplish.

Your actions must be consistent with your vision in order to reinforce it. Your thinking, feeling, and actions move up to where your vision is. Just as there are many steps in the development of a modern giant shopping center, so there are many steps in your demonstration. The architect's plan has to be reinforced by the action of the builder or contractor. Perhaps property has to be purchased, buildings leveled, before the materials are brought forth. Each such step reinforces the idea.

Don't let any false belief stand between you and your reinforcement. You cannot be successful while still thinking failure, nor can you be well while still thinking sickness. Whatever stands in the way must go. Success requires dynamic, positive ideas and action; so does health. Mental dormancy must go. Reinforce the divine idea by conforming to its pattern in all your thinking. Modern methods with giant bulldozers have eliminated the spade and shovel. Through scientific mental treatment, tremendous demonstrations eliminate time and space and make old trial-and-error methods obsolete.

Reinforce your vision by knowing that rightness is sustained. Perceive divine order. Recognize that all things are working together. Keep your thinking positive and dynamic. Be constructive. Don't give power to beliefs in delay or uncertainty. You have the ability to make decisions wisely and the stick-to-itiveness to carry through.

Every expedition or endeavor has a spearhead or advance guard that the follow-ups must be able to keep up with. Progress is measured by the actual working body, not by the spearhead— the construction workers digging foundations and putting up

115

steel frameworks, not the architect drawing up blueprints. Your idea must manifest in your outward expression. The vision of health or success must be reinforced by the actual appearance and expression of health and success. What you have in mind must be reinforced by what you do and by your fully completed demonstration.

Confidence without Arrogance

THE SCIENCE OF MIND stresses the importance of self-confidence and that man must learn to depend on a principle that will never fail him. All feelings of inferiority can be negated and all timidity can be wiped out. Underconfidence, on the other hand, can be a great problem, and the individual who undersells himself can be a great sufferer.

At the opposite end of this mental spectrum, you find the individual who is overconfident, becoming arrogant. How can students of the Science of Mind be overconfident? By presuming to be that which they have not yet unfolded the ability to be. A person may act prematurely or step into a position for which he or she has not yet qualified himself. Yet, the Science of Mind says you can do anything you want.

Evidently there is a balanced or middle course that you can choose. To be sure, you can be whatever you want to be, provided you qualify yourself to be that. In order to be an opera-singer, you would have to provide the voice and personality that could handle the opera. If you desire greater wealth, you must equip yourself mentally with the consciousness of great wealth. A tremendous mental equivalent must be acquired. Ernest Holmes, in *The Science of Mind*, says, "If you cannot walk on water, take a boat." Whatever you want to be, you have to equip yourself mentally, emotionally, and physically to be.

The answer to your dilemma is that both ends of the spectrum suffer from the same cause. The underconfident and the overconfident have the same mental desires or basic feelings of inadequacy. The underconfident person shows lack of initiative. This person expects to be forgiven for not making better progress. "You can't expect more from the poor dear." The overconfident person tends to throw out a smoke screen to prevent people seeing his or her own feeling of insecurity.

117

Your answer then is: Man is God Mind consciously expressing itself. Your thought must function on the God level, which
means that your God awareness establishes the equivalent of
God awareness in your expression in the outer world. True confidence means that you "deliver the goods." When you state
that you will succeed, you *know* that you will succeed, because
you will put into your world of expression all the endeavor
necessary to bring that success to pass.

Know What Is Involved

To SOME, LIFE seems to be a series of repeats, with people called back to complete what they should have done right the first time.

A comprehension of the situation involved reveals ways and means for doing it right. This attention is a *now* quality, applying your thought at the point where you are. No sense of time enters; no past and no future. The awareness of the present moment gives your attention its power. Don't let your mind lapse back to something that happened two hours before nor jump ahead to what you are going to do tomorrow. Become completely aware of who you are right now, the reality of this moment.

Your true self-recognition is the universal Mind knowing itself as you. There is no thought of growth or progress, and no thought of what has to be accomplished, but an identity of the self with infinite Intelligence at this very moment. In consciousness, you are not getting ready to do something nor trying to work something out. Your full attention is focused on the realization that the one Mind in you now knows all that you need to know and that its right knowingness is instantly manifest as immediate right action.

Recognize the greatness and immensity of this one Mind. It is truly omnipotent because there is nothing it cannot bring about. It dissolves erroneous beliefs. It wipes out frustrations. It brings such great illumination to your mind that you really see your individualized world as divine order.

Throughout the ages, men have experienced instantaneous healing. The most brutal and persistent persecutor of the Christians, Paul, was suddenly struck by the overpowering Presence of love and immediately became one of the greatest backers of the new religion. He was instantaneously healed of bigotry. People have been known to drop limitations like a lightning flash.

119

Man is instantly healed when he accepts the immensity of this power greater than himself. It makes its greatness felt by the person healed. All of these instances reaffirm that, when you rise in consciousness and recognize that you are one with all-powerful Mind, the perfection and wholeness of this Mind right this moment can become your experience. This awareness of nowness is called instantaneous healing.

Is There Always
a Better Way?

SINCE MIND IS infinite, Intelligence constantly produces new concepts to be acted upon. Every experience can be transcended. The thing you do today perhaps could be done better tomorrow. There must always be room for growth and expansion. However, a negative attitude about today can hamper this larger expression. Dissatisfaction does not necessarily inspire you into better action. Unhappiness in your present condition does not guarantee that you will change your method and produce happiness.

The law of growth begins where you are. It requires that your attitude of the present moment be constructive. The concept of something better must be induced into the present moment. Your thought must be lifted above the present situation in order to produce something better. Otherwise, your relationship with present conditions, desirable or undesirable, will have to remain the same.

Creativeness always anticipates that which you are not expressing at the present moment. The mental cause must precede its manifested effect. This is why practice does not necessarily make perfect. The musician may strike several wrong notes at the first reading of a composition, and he may also strike the same wrong notes a second and third time. A correction should be made at the first reading. This changes the pattern in a person's mind.

The law of growth requires a confrontation with your experience at the present moment. Evasion, whether it be self- or otherwise, is one of the greatest obstructions. But, equally, delay is emotional indignation over failure or inability to rise above a condition. It may seem much simpler to get mad or angry than to eliminate the cause of the negative experience. Each moment has something of truth to reveal to you. This does not mean that you accept a situation, if negative, in its entirety; however, there is a degree of truth manifesting. It is up to you to perceive what it is and to act on it. Perhaps the very feeling of dissatisfaction is the truth of your greater potential trying to make itself realized by you.

You need a new vision where you are to lift yourself into a new expression. Mentally, you must complete all that goes with your present situation. You are where you are because a life purpose has placed you there. Don't evade it or deny it. Only then will the better way appear.

Your Inspiration Never Diminishes

VISION HAS A WONDERFUL way of renewing itself, and inspiration greater than you have ever had before has a way of suddenly appearing. It is the age-old realization that life never diminishes its flow nor diverts its creative direction. Even in what you sometimes think are fallow periods, this great creative impulse of the universe would seem to be more intense than ever. The Infinite doesn't release its ideas until it is ready to have them fulfilled. No one comes before his time. You live in the era to which you belong. The ideas you have are not too advanced for the race. They have come in the fullness of season, and their rightness bounds forth without hindrance.

You do not always see this continuous action of infinite Mind. You generally see only certain points of expression or peaks of manifestation. You may measure waves from one crest to another, but the trough is a part of them. It is not really a downward movement but is part of the rhythmic action of the whole. There is never a moment in which you are outside this all-embracing creativeness of God. There is never a moment when the Presence is withdrawn from you. You are always inseparably one with it.

Your tendency is to measure your experiences only from wave crest to wave crest or from the moments of exalted meditation to exalted meditation. However, all the action in-between is a definite part of that which you experience. What would a high-rise building be without its foundation? When you see an excavation going down six or eight stories, it makes you realize that the foundation is just as exalted as the penthouse that surmounts it.

What you are thinking in your odd moments is a definite part of the mental action when you speak your word in treatment. Everything you think between lectures and classes and treatment periods is a necessary part of your great experience of being. Don't divide your time, thinking, and money, but recognize that you are a unitary whole and are not just the sum total of all of your attributes. You are the coordination and adhesiveness of these states of mind which maintain your identity in the one Intelligence—*always*.

Opportunities,
Not Challenges

AT TIMES SOME people have to be forced to move into a larger expression. It would seem that the universe is constantly challenging them or goading them into doing something new. When you understand the principle of life itself, you do not have to be goaded, coerced, or challenged. The acceptance of your place in the universal order reveals to you abilities and talents that cannot be suppressed. Limitless power at the center of your being will burst beyond your control into a new creative expression.

Basically, this divine urge within you is to expand its own divinity; therefore it is creative, constructive, and directive. It is no great effort for you to get started in a new adventure or experience when you recognize the nature of this inner drive. This recognition supersedes all psychological drives and emotional analysis. Such tangential experiences are left behind because all of your energy is focused upon this reality of your spiritual nature.

The Intelligence that endowed you with the power to be that which you are has fortified you and is always revealing to you ideas that will bring forth that expression. When people hesitate and have difficulty making up their minds, it is because they are thinking from a psychological point of view or living in their emotional feelings. When you are conscious of your spiritual reality and your identity in infinite Intelligence, there is no need to wait or postpone. You need to train yourself to be more perceptive; to be quicker in recognizing the power in new ideas.

Just because a new inspiration is sudden and catches you by surprise, it should not disarm you. The unawakened person has a defense mechanism that prevents seeing the power in the new idea. "Let's wait; let's not move too fast," is this person's reply. Spirit does not grab you by the shoulders and say, "Now listen! Do this!'' Intuition works so quietly and silently, almost subtly, that you have to be very alert and receptive to get it. It doesn't keep repeating itself. It speaks with an emphasis the il- lumined can understand, for intuition never forces or coerces. Intuition never makes you do anything. Opportunity is an inner recognition and acceptance that brings the complete release of ability and power.

Affirmations and Denials

IN BUILDING A HOUSE, you would start with your desire; then you would get the finest architect you could find and let him work on your idea. Perhaps before this you would have bought a lot. You may have gotten a beautiful lot but it may have had undesirable buildings on it. That would have been no problem, as your contractor could quickly clear the lot. He could move the obstruction and make way for your new idea.

You work to create what you want and to get rid of what you don't want. You work on your positive idea and eradicate all ideas contrary to it. This latter you call *denial*. Affirmations and denials, no matter by what name you call them, are the modus operandi of metaphysics. Your vision of what you want becomes your affirmation. Clearing your consciousness of mental obstruction becomes the denial.

Treatment begins with the affirmation. You affirm there is only one Mind and that Mind is your mind now. Now you affirm that your desired house is a perfect idea in God Mind. Everything necessary for its complete manifestation is now established: the right lot, the right architect, the right builder, the right financing. *All* is in divine order. That is your affirmation.

The denial is actually an affirmation also. The lot is properly surveyed. It is leveled and cleared of all obstructions. There are no buildings on it; no delays in clearing and grading; no delay in materials. There is no belief in any kind of obstruction, physical or financial. This constitutes a denial. Always follow a denial with an affirmation. For instance:

"Nothing can interfere with my good
because God is all-powerful."

Where you seem very conscious of the negative, specific work must be done. For instance, a negative growth:

127

"The power of God is the only power. There is no false growth, no tumor, no obstruction. The power of this word dissolves and removes anything unlike perfect God. There is no obstruction because God is the only power and there is no obstruction in God."

Another example, in the face of a seeming cold:

"There is no cold, because Spirit is not subject to heat or cold. Positive being is established and maintained in divine order."

A pinch of salt dropped on a large snail or slug will dissolve it. This is the way your denial works, only the denial acts on your consciousness. It dissolves the negative belief in you. Your mind is cleared exactly as the lot had to be cleared. You cannot establish new ideas when your mind is cluttered any more than you can build on top of the undesired outbuilding.

Another example of affirmation and denial:

"There is no procrastination and no one to believe in it [denial], for God is always on time, always where God wants to be when God wants to be there [affirmation]."

Don't neglect your denials, especially when a negative appearance seems to be there. Its visibility implies negative belief. You remove the outer by dissolving the belief that caused it and building up completely the perfect idea. Denial destroys the negative belief. Affirmation brings forth the truth and destroys the false negative belief. Affirmations are your creative consciousness at work. Denials are getting false beliefs out of the way.

Maneuverability

IT MAY SEEM a long road with no turning, but keep going and eventually it or you will turn. The Air Corps used to have a training field at Forth Worth and another at Dallas. One of the students could take off nicely but could not make a turn in the air. So he flew in a straight line, landed at Fort Worth, turned his plane around, and flew back in a straight line to Dallas. That is learning the hard way.

In other words, maneuverability is a necessary qualification for accomplishment. You cannot always go in a straight line, and if the road does not seem to turn, you make your own turns. It is amazing how many years some people drive an automobile and yet never learn the simple operation of parking a car. You learn to maneuver and develop different ways of doing everything you do, yet you still adhere to your principle.

God is the only power and operates through the creativeness of Mind. All that you do is the action of this creative Mind. This Mind, thinking as you, must be flexible. It not only creates unpredictable experiences, but it is called upon to act in all kinds of unanticipated experiences. Turning around does not mean retreating, nor does parking an automobile mean the end of the day. The basic principle of life is progressive. There are times to act positively and aggressively, and there are times to be quiet and meditative. There are times when you push forward as rapidly as possible. There are other times when you stand still. To live without tension and to operate without pressure is your goal. This enables you to do your best work.

These inner states continually reflect your own awareness. Water seldom moves in a straight line, nor does it circle unnecessarily. It follows the line of least resistance. Your greatest problem in life is to get rid of the resistance—beliefs that resist progress and change, habits that have so gripped you that you

129

forget how they were originally started. Emerson says, "In one direction, every door is open." The water creates its own channels and establishes its own banks. You project your ability and create your own receptivity. Your inner perception knows no obstacle and countenances no negativity.

Change: Good or Bad?

CHANGE, JUST FOR the sake of change, is not necessarily constructive. Principle itself does not change. God, divine Principle, infinite Intelligence, is eternally the same. This is the basis of your philosophy. The expression of infinite Principle is constantly undergoing change, but its action is always constructive. Its changes reflect a larger concept whose time has come. It is an expanded awareness projecting itself as larger opportunity. The conscious creator controls all change so that relationships do not disentegrate nor conditions deteriorate. Only when the ideas back of the experience have expended themselves is it time to move on.

Change, just for the sake of change, can become a mania. This is due to a lack of inner security. It is a blind frenzy striking in every direction, subconsciously hoping that the right direction might thus be found. But growth comes only through conscious choice, and changes should be those that you consciously make. This means that you know why you are taking a stand, what it is you expect to work out, and why you are so certain that the energy of the old idea has expended itself.

When you feel yourself caught or trapped in a situation, you are confronted with the necessity to change. When a Broadway play has proven itself and is running successfully, the rule is, don't change it. No matter how many times the producer is tempted to improve it, it is left alone. The writer also edits and re-edits, erases and adds to what has been written, making all kinds of changes. But the moment comes when all of a sudden he or she knows that nothing else should be changed. Although ideas will continue to flow, the writer learns to accept what has been written. Unfortunately, people can pick on themselves and become very petty analyzing their motives and questioning their actions. Perhaps every success can be outdone. But when an idea

131

reaches a certain point, it must run its course. The wise person knows when to stand still.

This complete acceptance makes the demonstration. Then you are ready for a larger experience. Each step you take is necessary and must be accepted before you can move on. Although life and Principle do not change, your experiences cannot stand still.

Why Didn't I Think of That?

You ARE A CENTER of creative Intelligence whose progress depends upon personal initiative. The Science of Mind is a participating activity—not a spectator study. It challenges you to do something new or different. Success requires initiative. The successful business executive seeks to expand the business. New products must be made available and new methods of distribution developed.

This is why it is important to work within your own consciousness. You are part of an infinite Intelligence; you are one with Mind that knows. That Mind is all-revealing at the level of your receptivity. A new way never opens to the person that is thoroughly satisfied with what he or she is doing now. Nor does it generally open for the person that is grumbling and complaining. To expand, you accept the good that you have and, using your initiative, you will ensure continuous renewal and increase. You become mentally receptive to the new ideas that will bring this increase about.

Perhaps every invention has been due to humanity's desire to bring about greater efficiency. Through the automobile, we can get to our destination more quickly. The same is true of the jet or the supersonic plane. Spiritually, we want to take less time to arrive at inner peace and tranquillity and to spend less time in doing what we have to do. This is where creative Mind comes into action. The inventions that make life easier are instances of creative Mind at work.

Initiative gets you into action. It poses questions: How can you be more successful? What can you do to be saved from unpleasantness and difficulties? The answer is in your mental acceptance of creative Mind at work. Your consciousness of efficiency can get rid of procrastination and slovenliness. Your consciousness of right knowing can bring vital information to you. The realization of the one all-knowing Mind in you gets rid of doubt and uncertainty. You can develop initiative. Shyness and timidity are challenges to move into new experiences. Whatever has been thought or produced by anyone, no matter how brilliant the idea, can be equaled or surpassed by you. What if you *are* fearful—so what? Get going!

Happy Thinking
for a Happy Year!

YOUR MIND IS THE greatest power in your life. It operates according to understandable laws that you can depend on. Your study of the Science of Mind reveals laws that you can use to control your life and bring order into every area.

It is not always easy to figure where ideas come from. You are not always responsible for the ideas that you seemingly attract. The Science of Mind shows how you can regulate your thinking. It teaches how not to let in undesirable thoughts. What comes into your mind has no power over you unless you make it a part of your conscious thinking.

Positive thinking must be purposeful, constructive thinking in order to be effective. Undesirable thoughts and fears can also be very positive. The easiest way to keep out of your mind and experience those ideas which you do not want to express is to be definite and consistent in thinking what you do want and to work to that end. A positive image of your successful self automatically dispels any negative suggestions that might come to you. You are not held accountable for what you do not think, but you are responsible for what you do think and accomplish.

Controlled thinking is directional thinking. The Intelligence within you knows what you can be most effective in doing. This Intelligence also knows that it is not a hit-and-miss proposition, but one of definite, consecrated attention.

As with any scientific study, understanding Science of Mind is an art. Emerson said that the most difficult thing in the world is to think. Systematic study and research into how your mind functions will give you your greatest power. The mental image of you in your right place, in your right environment, doing your right work, becomes the focal point at which infinite Intelligence expresses. The Science of Mind is the art of thinking correctly about yourself, your ability, and life, so that what you do expresses fully what you know.

135

On Spring

As INEVITABLY AS NIGHT and day follow each other, so the completion of your mental demonstration is followed by new ideas and new opportunities. This eternal cycle always fulfills itself. Mind can never run out of ideas. Neither can your intelligence be exhausted.

Sometimes it is difficult to know where or when an experience is ended and a new one begins. The river flows imperceptibly into the sea; the boy grows into manhood. The continuous process of creativeness makes it difficult to perceive stages in what you are doing. Few people can perceive their growth. You cannot place your finger on the exact turning-point from difficulty into ease of expression, nor can you see when someone turns from frustration to success.

When a person moves from one location to another or buys a new factory or store, that is only the outer manifestation. The turning point is in mind when that person begins to think differently about him- or herself.

You think *into* your demonstration to make it come to pass. Your dominant thought will motivate you. Visions of how it is going to unfold will enthuse you. Then you will think in terms of the actually completed demonstration, and you will act mentally as though it had already occurred. Every change in a person's life is a change of thought, a change of mind. No one can see it coming; no one knows when it is going to happen; but when the person inwardly makes up his or her mind, that is when it happens. It is silent mental working beyond your range of vision.

Perhaps this means that winter would be more important than spring. It is in the dormancy of winter that impending life is pulled together, organized, and focused. Spring tells you that it has already happened. So does your demonstration. Credit goes to the decision that you made in silence and to the inner determination that changed your trend of thinking. Spring is the acknowledgment in nature that the silent work of winter was effective. And so your demonstration is the acknowledgment in the outer world that your silent creation was real. Spring comes because of what took place in winter.

It Is Your Reward

THE AGE-OLD CYCLE of sowing and reaping, planting and harvesting, cause and effect, represents the eternal verity that life ever maintains its cycle of knowing and being, thinking and expressing. But sometimes the harvest is neglected. The apples remain on the tree. The guavas are never picked. The good that you create is never utilized. Harvest is important, because it represents a completion of the cycle.

Your creativeness must manifest. What you think must be your experience. This is a law of being. It must be clearly understood: When you speak your word, something happens. But make sure your consciousness is there at the happening. Your treatment does work. Make sure you see the working of your treatment.

The effect of the treatment may not be according to your photographic mental image, but it will contain all of the elements of your treatment. You may never have seen the blossom of the rare, exotic bulb that you purchase at the nursery, and you may not know what its blossom will look like. Its blossom, when it appears, may be completely foreign to your concept of it; but the bulb cannot change to oblige your imagination. It has a law within itself and therefore must produce according to its own law of being.

This same thing is true of your treatment. Each treatment has its law which cannot be violated. Your treatment cannot break this law in order to fulfill your imagination. An intelligent understanding of treatment will prevent disappointment. You must recognize what must go into the treatment to bring out that which is desired. Therefore, you learn to give treatments that include what is consistent with your desire and what does not violate the nature of the treatment itself. This understanding will simplify your treatment method.

The law doesn't work because of your profundity. The law is a very simple one. As you think, believing and accepting, the creative cause is established, and the effect will follow. Put into your treatment what you want to come out of it. Give it in peace, harmony, and joy—because you want peace, harmony and joy to come out of it.

Successful treatment brings successful fulfillment, not as a reward but as an inevitable consequence. The farmer is not rewarded for his faithfulness, but the cycle is fulfilled. What he sows, he reaps. This is the wondrous manifestation of Law.

Principles Expanded

One Power

GOD IS THE ONLY power that heals regardless of what form of therapy an individual might use. The physician, surgeon, dentist, practitioner, and minister are avenues through which God expresses.

You have no criticism of any form of healing. No matter what the physical appearance might be, you find the real cause in mind. To change the condition in the body, you must change the pattern of your thinking. Body is an effect. The cause is in mind.

You are not mortal nor physical; you are spiritual Mind. You partake of the nature of God and are endowed with divine attributes. Your life has purpose, and every experience has meaning.

In order to be well, you must be conscious of filling your right place in life and must recognize the worthwhileness of your expression. Spiritual healing is the recognition of this truth. The great Master associated health with wholeness. You must function as an integrated whole being. You must recognize the inner completeness of your spiritual life.

To be consciously at one with God is to be at peace. To recognize God as the Presence within you eliminates all discord and strife. To know that your God Love fills you is to create a deeper understanding in all of your relationships in life. God *is* the healing power. With God all things are possible. Sickness, sin, or limitation cannot endure in the healing Presence.

Power Unlimited

Your spiritual horizon is constantly expanding. Your personal power is attained through the use of Principle, and this applies equally to all people. No one has a peculiar access to truth. No one has God-ordained insight into why people prosper and why they are happy. These experiences are based upon Principle, which all can use.

Of course you are interested in your individual demonstration. It should mean more to you than anything else in the world. Each wants to express the highest and greatest good. If this desire is based only on your individual effort and interest, it will lack power. When you link up your effort with this universal Principle in action, its power will become unlimited. Each must know what can be done personally, and yet to that attitude should be added the recognition that all people can do the same thing. This keeps the power in Principle. Others have only to recognize the power and use it.

You are endowed with a divine Something. If the power depends upon personal possessions, then fear might come in. Someone might take away from you what belongs to you, or you might find yourself frantically trying to get what someone else has. But Principle makes you realize that your own comes to you because you recognize it and claim it. Each person draws that which is recognized and claimed. No one is really free until all are free. Your Science of Mind teaching is the most inclusive in the world. The one Mind maintains its oneness of being in all persons everywhere. No one receives more than all others can also receive when this truth is known and perceived. Always stay in Principle.

The Infinite You

WHILE TRUTH IS eternally the same and never changes, the outward world of appearance changes constantly. Principles are eternal, but we are ever finding new methods of applying them. Through your belief you utilize changeless principles. Ideas or mental concepts give this changeless Mind its outward propulsion. So progress and change are linked together.

However, merely to change for the sake of changing does not necessarily denote progress, for every constructive change should be the fulfillment of a pattern. You should be motivated by your determination to fulfill a design or carry out a plan. Everything must first be thought of before it can be produced.

Change that denotes progress is not just a rearrangement of the same old facts or regrouping of the same old experiences. Progressive change brings something new into the consciousness of the individual, just as the third grade at school is not a repetition or a duplication of the second grade, but represents the gathering together of new knowledge. Your mind is infinite; therefore, to grow you cannot become set in your ways or become a creature of habit. Such false concepts interfere with the spiritual progress of the self. You are infinite Mind; therefore, each day must bring new ideas, a new knowledge, and a new opportunity for establishing better conditions in every phase of living.

You Are Your World

YOU PLACE THE VALUE on what you do. It is a personal appraisal. That which seems trivial to one could be world-binding to another. The sports fan can live in a world unfathomable to the nonsportsman. The artist and the musician enter into a world made known only to them. Each one has a Holy of Holies. The Infinite speaks only according to your understanding; Spirit reveals itself at the level of your understanding and comprehension. This is why the unenlightened imagines that there are many gods. The secrets of science are unlocked to those who can comprehend. But never to the profane.

Spirit will reveal its depths to you when you are ready. Think the thoughts of God and speak the language of God. Thus only you can enter your Holy of Holies.

You Create Your World

YOUR EXPERIENCE IN LIFE should be the joyous unfoldment of your God-Self in all its power. Life is not a probationary period, nor is it a school of discipline. It is an opportunity to develop your creativeness and, through scientific right thinking, make your world the kind of a world that you want to live in.

God has endowed you with creative power. Therefore you cannot spend your time on the receiving end waiting for things to happen. You are co-creator with God. Your thinking and feeling must be unified with God Mind and God Love. There is no substitute for spiritual initiative in every phase of your human expression. Utilize the power that God has given you. The right of choice must not be restricted to a rejection of what you do not want but must find its full concentrated force in creating what you do want. You can create the kind of world that you want to live in.

Life Is for Living

LIFE IS TO BE lived. You do not know what life is. It cannot be measured or defined. You know it only through your livingness.

You also know that its nature is expansive. It is free from restrictions and apparently only wants to be more of itself. Like the wind which you cannot see, you observe its effect and what it does around you.

The more you look for aliveness, the more alive you seem to be. Your aliveness manifests in your wealth and in your successful ventures. Your health seems to jump forward in great leaps as you realize life is for living. Your joy overflows. Your love is unbounded. You are life living prosperously. You are life living its well-being. You are life ever being more alive—fully itself.

Live Up to Your Freedom

FREEDOM AND BONDAGE are states of mind. You are subject to your belief about yourself and the universe around you. Since Mind is creative, that which you believe will become your experience. Whatever thought dominates your mind will inevitably become your experience. It will color your thinking, creep into your conversation, and govern your relationship with those around you.

If your dominant mind is constructive and adds to your well-being, it will bring you freedom to express. Develop wonderful power of expression and keen insight into opportunities in life. Don't personally enslave yourself.

No negative condition need last any longer than the thinking that created it. Neither bondage nor freedom is a state of mind that is attained once and for all. You are a growing, evolving individual, and the experiences that you have reflect this growth. Consequently, each day your decisions will perpetuate the freedom that you have proven, or they will tighten the bondage that you have accepted. You were born free and endowed by the infinite Creator with the ability to be self-creating and self-sustaining. You are the master of your universe. You must know this and accept it.

The Resistless Urge

HOPE AND FAITH are eternally made new. Regardless of the experiences you may find yourself in, hope will always stir you and faith will call forth a new effort on your part. You cannot be inactive for very long. Life itself is always seeking expression through you.

You could not be any other way, because the life you are is infinite. The law of your life is one of eternal progression. Constantly you will be challenged to a larger fulfillment of yourself.

No matter how difficult the situation may be, hope never gives up. It operates independently of your will, or thoughts, or desires. It is the spirit of God. This can never die. This divine urge constantly pulls your mind away from any bondage to external conditions and centers it on the creativeness of your God self.

Hope and faith are imperishable, because the life that you are is God, and God can never die. Neither can you—the Real you.

Make a Fresh Start

THE GREATEST THING in life is to discover who you are and why you are where you are today. Mind, or consciousness, is the great reality. You live intelligently in a world governed by Intelligence.

While you may in some respects be the product of your past, that must be forgotten. You must rise above that conception. Life is constantly starting new endeavors. The past is gone. Your true spiritual discernment knows only beginnings—all things new. Not as a moving picture passing upon a screen but as an active involvement. It is not a passing experience but such a real involvement that it knows no past and no future. Your concern and participation are so deep and far-reaching that you feel yourself at the center of all that is or all that ever could be.

You are one with the Source of all that is. You function even as the Source. The people in your life you meet at that Source. All that will ever be are experiences that you have at that Source. This is that which was in the beginning, is now, and ever shall be. This the mystics, the spiritual progenitors, have always known. You, the modern mystic, no longer function in a world of ignorance. You were born into the light. Your way is clear. You are being now where you are.

Self-Contemplation

YOUR BASIC PRINCIPLES are very simple.

The only reality is God, creative Spirit, Mind.

This is First Cause and the only substance there is.

God is all intelligence and operates through each individual's thought.

Your mind is the point of focus.

You have access to all the Substance there is.

Substance is formless but becomes to you the form that you think into it.

It works through a law of subjectivity that accepts your idea and conviction and produces it as your experience.

God acts only through the self and proclaims its oneness with you.

You identify yourself with the nature of the Divine.

Through your power of choice, you think Substance into the form your experiences will take.

Infinite Mind reproduces its own nature as its creation.

Each person is the result of the self-contemplation of Spirit.

In order to express this, you must sustain your thinking at the level of God-knowing.

God reproduces the consciousness of God as your true nature and duplicates its reproductive process in you as your method of creation.

You become the experience you envision.

You Are the Pilot

PERIODICALLY YOU STOP to measure your ability and check your resources so you can clarify your thoughts about the direction you are going in. Generally you are so busy and involved in what you are doing that you may forget the details or do not have time to check them.

A commercial jetliner has three or four persons in the cockpit, all of them busy. Seldom do you ask for assistance in your personal life. It is all up to you; yet, as your solo pilot, you have many points of assistance. Your intuition opens untold doors in your perception. This informing intelligence never fails. Your subjective mind is constantly accepting your thought commands. It works on them while your conscious mind moves into other areas. You develop the ability to see mental causes where others may see only appearances or effects. You develop the mental capacity to choose and stick to your choice. You learn to apply pressure where it is effective—that is, within your consciousness. You do not let conditions affect you. You become immune to outside influences.

The purpose of this study in self-awareness is to appraise your ability not only to resist pressures but to create what you really want. When you know this, you are ready to take over the complete command—captain, pilot, copilot, and navigator.

Chart Your Course

YOU HAVE THE POWER to create good experiences. This results from the right use of mental law. What you contemplate tends to objectify itself as your experience. Consequently, you should give your attention only to those ideas that you want to express. Criticism and fault-finding should occupy no place in your thinking or conversation.

Instead, you should establish a deep faith in Good. When negative or fear thoughts appear, you can reject them and consciously choose their opposites. You can make your consciousness of Good so strong that only right action will take place.

This principle you do not compromise. You do not call half a loaf a loaf, nor suffering and despair Good. Your consciousness of Good will create experiences that will be constructive. Good experiences must increase your well-being and add to your livingness.

To sustain Good, you must formulate ideas that will produce Good. You must take the initiative. Just as every jet flight is charted beforehand, so you must know where you are going. You shall become like that to which you devote your attention. Progress, success, love, and peace are all created in mind. When you accept them in consciousness you give them expression.

Be Versatile

KEEP FAITH WITH YOUR secret desires. Your dreams, your aspirations, your hopes are meaningful and important. They must see the light of day. Believe in your unseen ability and develop your hidden talents. Make your dreams come true.

Your major decision—your life's work or profession—should dominate your thinking, and rightly so. Subconscious law works relentlessly to achieve this.

But in addition to this powerful expression, everyone needs a special, active hobby. This can offer a diversion that will broaden your vision and expand your talents. It must be constructive, intensely interesting, and challenging.

This side-activity will give your major expression a breather. You will return to it with fresh vision and new energy. These extracurricular hobbies will sharpen your perception and add depth to your major endeavor. Believe greatly and prove that you really know.

Change Your Pace

LEAVING TOWN AND GOING to a foreign country does not necessarily constitute a vacation. Wondering about your business and being concerned with your family can carry the same mental state you had at home. A vacation is a change of pace and change of thought. You leave your work and family, knowing that nothing can happen to them. They will be there when you return.

Some pre-vacation exercises will help prepare you. In treatment or prayer, you center your attention on your God Being. You shut out distractions and close the door on outer experiences. You draw on the one Presence. You see your divine Reality. You build into consciousness what you want to experience. This changes your pace. You drop, for the time being, the daily situation and create the new.

> When thou prayest, enter into thy closet,
> and when thou hast shut thy door,
> pray to thy Father which is in secret,
> and thy Father which seeth in secret
> shall reward thee openly.

Sustain Order

THERE IS AN INTELLIGENCE in the universe that governs and maintains order. It operates in your life at the level of consciousness where you are. Consequently, when you know that God Mind is all-revealing, you create a receptivity through which the God Intelligence can express. Your positive conviction that there is a Power that responds to you always brings it forth. Whatever demand you make in consciousness is always met. God action makes your life orderly. A positive force for good operates in your thinking, feeling, and acting. Its unfailing directive power gives you confidence and assurance.

Avoid letting your mind become cluttered with unnecessary details. Divine Intelligence includes everything necessary for whatever project you undertake. Details will automatically fall into line when you consciously know that divine order governs. Every step will work out harmoniously and effectively. Divine Intelligence will include the right emphasis on each detail. The importance of the overall pattern will always be stressed. Divine Intelligence will keep this in mind.

No Pressure

THE UNIVERSE IS not under pressure; neither are you. Life is law operating through love. The baby chick comes out of its shell when it is ready. There is no force. The fruit falls when it ripens.

Your spiritual rhythm is not under pressure. You do not have to do anything until you are ready.

At this point, the Law operates with certainty and yet almost with a restraint. Something seems to say, "Take your time—easy does it—don't push. Let it be."

Come unto me, all ye that labor . . . for my yoke is easy, and my burden is light.

Spirit does not shout. It does not push or coerce. It is a still, small voice. A quiet inner knowing.

When you stop pushing and fighting and shouting, in the stillness of your being you will proclaim yourself.

Take It Easy

STEADFASTNESS OF FAITH results from practice. It is part of your spiritual growth. This does not mean that you will never doubt or that your mind will never wander. Perhaps no one has ever arrived at that place. Since Mind is infinite and you are constantly receiving new mental impulses, many new trains of thought will open for you even in the midst of the most serious study.

Any system of mental concentration would destroy this mental receptivity. You do not want to become rigid in your mental outlook. If the mind wanders, bring it gently back to the dominant point of attention. You can never force yourself to think about anything, nor can you use willpower to gain mental growth. The greater the mental interest, the more steadfast will you be.

It is very difficult to hold the mind very long on ideas that have no appeal to you. If you are interested and happy in your work, you can accomplish your task with a minimum of effort. Whatever ideas you choose for your experience must appeal to you. Even many things that you do through a sense of duty will interest you when you understand what is involved.

Everyone should be well, happy, loving, and prosperous. These four basic interests are common to all, but each concept must have a vital place in your mental plan. As you work in this definite way you will find that your mind will be sharp and that your mental approach will be decisive and sure. This habit will establish steadfastness.

You Control Consciousness

YOUR ONLY CHALLENGE in life is to stop looking at outer conditions as power objects or symbols and to recognize the unlimited, unformed creative consciousness which you are.

You should live in a world of beauty and opulence, but what you are is greater than what you demonstrate. It is this limitless consciousness of your unmanifested thinking that challenges you. Your desire and your thought give this unformed mind-substance its form. What you think of yourself is accepted by Spirit. You create your conviction of being it. What you conceive in mind is manifest in your outer world.

Your idea has power. You can produce what you desire. Just as the seed that has creative power must be placed in its creative medium, the soil, so your idea must remain in consciousness. Let your ideas finish themselves. Each completed idea makes way for a new idea. Life cannot be stopped. You cannot stop living. Are you maintaining the quality of conciousness you want to sustain? Your life does have meaning, but it must be consciously established. You are perfect, whole, and complete, but you must know it.

No one can grow spiritually for you any more than another person can eat for you. No one can solve a problem for you or make you rich or poor. Only you.

You have access to the wisdom of the ages. There is no messiah nor seer to give you the answer you want. Only you can meet your challenges. And you can.

Your Cycle of Progression

WHILE SEASONS COME and go, and your individual experiences wax and wane, the eternal progression of universal goodness never ceases—never varies. It is the life in which you think and feel. Your innermost thoughts, your true creative power, have their source in this eternal flow of cosmic life.

Your material world, your emotions, and your body are outer expressions of thought. The Self unfolds as spiritual Mind. All cause is seen in consciousness. Your thought chooses your experiences. Emotional balance and mental composure sustain self-control.

The poised self can proclaim its oneness with universal Mind. Its balance affords the cosmic Force a point at which it can sustain its self-awareness and self-expression.

The bondage of matter is broken when you transcend your belief that you are governed by circumstances and conditions. You are spiritual Mind—a spiritual being in a spiritual world. This awareness or consciousness is the true cause of all that is.

Make Up Your Mind

MIND IS YOUR greatest discovery. Your use of Mind is the greatest power in your possession. Through your understanding of the way in which Mind works, you can create in your life the conditions that you desire.

Mind is unlimited in its nature, and its possibilities are inexhaustible. It operates in you and through the law of your belief. It accepts your belief and creates it as your experience. Your beliefs are self-imposed and self-accepted. You have the power to reject anything you do not want to believe. You can even reject the truth. Any belief in inadequacy or frustration is the self-rejection of truth.

Your finances follow the pattern of your belief; so do opportunity and success. Your life in its entirety is governed by what you believe. Great persons believe in their limitless possibilities. They are not afraid to make extravagant demands upon themselves. They expect to do the impossible. Their belief justifies their assumption, and they accomplish the difficult task they set out to attain.

Your belief may change from time to time. What you believe is determined by what you think. Your dominant thought will become your belief. Consequently, you determine your belief by the way in which you control your thought. You are infinite Mind, with limitless possibilities. What you make up your mind to be, you will be.

Reality of Your Vision

VISIONS OR DREAMS? Both. Your dream turns into your vision through understanding the law of creative Mind. What you think about you become when you know that your vision acts upon creative Substance. Until you invoke this law, your dream is content to be an air castle or a daydream.

Ideas come from the mind because you are mind and it is also where you function. These ideas can "come to pass," or pause to become your tangible experience. The inventor is not the only one to whom the inventive idea appears. It comes to many all over the world, but the one who first latches onto it becomes the inventor, making it his or her idea. The same is true of the artist or the poet or the writer. If you don't use the idea, someone else will. It does not come to you on an exclusive wavelength. It is broadcast universally and simultaneously on all bands. Hundreds or thousands could tune in on it—if they would listen.

Watch your dream. Let it develop so that you dream on. Suddenly—in a moment, in the twinkling of an eye—you will grab your dream. Then, as vision, it will move into action. "See what God hath wrought."

Belief Comes First

THE SCIENCE OF MIND teaches a spiritual mental law that responds to your thought. Demonstration means using this law to fulfill your needs. What you think about yourself acts upon this universal mental law.

Demonstration is very simple, but it involves very definite mental laws. It responds to your belief. It heals according to your belief. It prospers you according to your belief. Your belief becomes the thing you think about. As long as you believe that you cannot, your belief holds you back. As you change your belief, conditions around you change.

The belief precedes the manifestation. Where you may feel there is no justifiable evidence for your belief in success, when you center your consciousness on success—think it, feel it, talk about it, and keep out doubts and negative suggestions—your belief in your desire will begin to grow. You will get stronger and stronger.

Believe in this infinite Mind responding to you. Believe that life loves you, respects you, and wants you to prosper.

Believe in this all-powerful Spirit. Then believe in yourself. What if you have had difficulties or even failures? Get them out of your consciousness. Believe in this moment. Believe that now you are the beloved of God and the heir to the kingdom, and your belief will be established unto you.

You Choose

PURPOSE GIVES MEANING to whatever you do. Life challenges you to be your best. Merely to be average is not good enough; that represents the mass mind. Individuality takes you beyond that; it breaks the hold that race mind exerts. As the astronauts go beyond the law of gravity, so a positive dynamic purpose goes beyond the race consciousness.

Purpose is individual and personal. You are endowed with the right of choice and discrimination. You have a built-in power that enables you to achieve your desire. The intensity of your desire and the sincerity of your actions give you your power, and a cosmic force backs up your effort.

As you commit yourself to accomplish your purpose, your vision broadens. New incentives for action inspire you. You have the power available, and it responds to you when you call it forth.

Choose your purpose carefully. Make sure it reflects your conviction. Commit yourself wholeheartedly to it and mentally live in it.

Commit Yourself

GROWTH IS NOT a painful process. The only thing that you can learn through suffering is (1) that it does not have to be, and (2) how you can avoid it.

Growth is the enlargement of your consciousness—a new awareness of who you are, a new opportunity to expand your creativity. Every procedure is positive and constructive. You project your thought into new areas of expression.

Your progress is measured in terms of positive action—not what you refrain from or avoid, but what you are doing that provides an outlet for your creative energy. You become more efficient in what you do. You listen to what you hear. You involve yourself in every experience. Nothing moves without you. You are totally committed to the divine fulfillment.

Some growth indicators: You keep your cool and do not get emotionally agitated. You are in control and create experiences of poise and peace. You keep your mind in focus and do not scatter your energy. You are quick to appraise each situation and to know what it will cost to succeed. Growth brings spiritual enlightenment and reveals the truth of Being.

Act Your Belief

WHEN THINGS SEEM to be difficult, a change of attitude will bring a new look at your situation. Your attitude precedes your demonstration. Look through the unpleasant condition. It can reflect a negative attitude, but it does not represent what you really are. Don't get so involved in conditions that you forget who you really are. You may drive through a dense fog, but you are not the fog. The same is true of every experience. You are spiritual Mind in action. You are its perfect embodiment, but you have to know this.

How can you rise above the condition and be conscious of who you really are? Through thought. Pretend you are doing the best thing for you although you do not believe it. Affirm the all-ness of God—even in the face of doubt. Act mentally the way you want to be even though you feel the opposite.

Every time you affirm the truth of Being, something happens in your unseen world of Mind. Water can be cleansed by drop after drop of pure water being applied to it. Thought purifies in the same way. Suddenly you can be surprised to find that you actually believe wholeheartedly what you have been affirming.

This is the creative principle at work: Present the truth as an affirmation. Repeat the process. Begin to act out your desired belief. Before you know it and almost unawares, you find yourself expressing your desire. You no longer have to pretend. You are the thing itself. You have made your demonstration.

Welcome the New Idea

A NEW IDEA WILL always produce a new experience unless you interfere with it or fail to accept it. Each thing that you are doing today represents previous ideas. The events around you follow subconscious patterns. Each day should bring you new ideas regarding your possibilities and your work. Each new idea will create a new mold for its expression, therefore you should not try to force the new ideas into old forms of expression.

You may have to train yourself to release the old. Sometimes it seems difficult to know when an experience has completed itself, but more often you hold on to old experiences through fear. You are afraid of what will happen if you let the old experience go.

Through faith, you realize that whatever you release will be replaced by something greater. Each task well done makes way for a greater one. Whenever you tire of the old you can reach out for new ideas. New ideas will lift you out of monotonous or boring experiences and will create new ones.

The new idea must be received with joy. It must have joy in it in order to unfold as a joyous experience. All negation must be kept out of the new ideas. There must be no feeling of difficulty of attainment or fear of frustration in your new ideas. The intelligence that presented this new idea to you has sufficient power to bring it to its successful consummation. Mind is infinite. Intelligence is never at a standstill. You have only to get still mentally, become receptive, and new ideas will be revealed.

Believe in Your Ideas

WHEN YOU UNDERSTAND that all is Mind, there is only one way that you can really work: that is through ideas. Mind is infinite and limitless. The principle of Intelligence is inexhaustible; you can relate to it only through your thought as specific ideas. In order for Mind to be more than an abstraction to you, you present definite ideas to it.

This operation seems to be twofold. Mind acts as a great reservoir of all knowinginess, and it also acts as a subjective force that accepts the ideas with which it is impregnated and forms them as your experience. The only limit it knows is in your personal awareness. It can operate in you only at the level of your comprehension. Your vision and your sense of acceptance have to be within your range of understanding. You do not try to go over your head or beyond your capacity to understand.

Sometimes you may wonder if anything new can be produced. Your inventions seem very conclusive, yet you are in a new age. The computers and the satellites stagger the imagination. Truly, you are only on the threshold of great new beginnings.

Where does all this activity of science come from? It originates in Mind. Its effectiveness is Mind's projection. Its accomplishment is that which Mind decrees.

Your Mind and my Mind—the greatest power in the world. You are using it this very minute.

169

Don't Be Hard on Yourself

WHILE YOU ARE constantly seeking to improve everything you do, you must be very careful not to pick on yourself. The law of progress is not automatic and requires conscious acceptance of new ideas on your part. It demands new incentives, new vision.

In your own experience you do not like to have others pick on you, even for your own good. It creates resentment and a negative reaction. The same principle is true in self-progress. Do not do things just because it is good for you to do them. While it is necessary to discipline yourself, you cannot rule yourself with an iron hand or punish yourself for your transgressions. What you think about tends to blossom and grow.

The outer self is beautiful, precious, and sacred. It responds to your most tender feelings. Yet it knows when you are serious and mean business. It is the positive reenforcement of faith in Good that brings progress—a constant recognition that you are growing and are part of the Great Self itself. You are not humoring yourself. You are making it plain that you believe in your capacity and that you have the ability to produce what you want.

The Two Aspects of Treatment

MENTAL TREATMENT OR PRAYER has two aspects. First, your desire, which you consciously pray to have fulfilled, and second, how you think about the same desire after your formal prayer is over.

Choosing what you shall treat to have fulfilled is very important. This decision should be made with care, for it is such a waste of time to work for things that we do not really want. Anything that you really want merits the full support of your consciousness through your mental/spiritual act. Mind is the only creative power in the universe. Your attitude can cause either good or bad to appear. Consciously choose the way you want your life to be.

The second side of prayer is apt to be overlooked or rejected. Have faith that your prayer will be answered. Back up that faith by acting as though you believed it. Do not wonder when the demonstration is to be made. Every time you think about the demonstration you must affirm that your desire is fulfilled. This unconscious side of prayer, like the submerged part of an iceberg, carries the greater weight.

The two aspects must be brought together. Conscious thinking and subjective feelings must be unified. This is successful mental treatment.

Depend on the Law

UNIVERSAL PRINCIPLES ARE no respecters of persons. All principles respond alike to everyone. The difference is not in the way in which the Law works for each individual, but rather in the relationship that each establishes with the Law. For instance, an escalator maintains a constant direction. It does not change to conform to your desire. You can step aboard, stand still, and be carried up to another floor. You can, if the authorities are not watching, even walk down an escalator that is going up. It complicates your experience, but nevertheless it can be done. When you choose to go the way it goes, it appears to operate for you.

The principle of the Science of Mind in like manner works for you. Your dominant thought establishes your relationship with this principle. If you believe that life is against you and that you are lacking in opportunity, you establish a reverse relationship with the creative principle. You can still succeed, just as you can walk in the wrong direction on the moving stairway, but your success is attained under abnormal difficulty.

The nature of the creative principle is to create. You can expect to progress and you can think success. Your consciousness will then move in the same direction as the creative principle. Success belongs to you. It is right for you to prosper. To accept this with conviction causes all of your experiences to maintain their right relationship with the creative principle. The law works for you when you make yourself receptive to it.

Let the Law Work

YOU HAVE AN INSATIABLE desire to make your mark in the world. You are endowed with a creative power that can never rest or be dormant. This cosmic urge to *be* will never stop. Its movement never slows down. It carries you forward.

You can relax when you board a jetliner or a train. Your part is to get aboard, knowing the destination of your travel carrier. You choose your desires and ideas. The law of Mind takes over when you relax and leave Mind free to work out the ideas. You don't interfere with Principle. It knows how, is able and willing, and does its perfect work.

Your part is to choose personally what you want. No one can do that for you. You then relax and give the law of Mind complete freedom to do its work. You keep faith with it and it keeps faith with you.

Don't Mentally
Jump the Gun

CREATIVE MIND OPERATES with such simplicity that many people overlook it. Your thought operates through a universal medium of Mind. This is the creative principle. What you think is accepted by this subjective mind and produced as form. There is no limit as to what you can do. It is all a matter of what you include in your consciousness. How much good can you think about or envision? Something happens every time you think. Every time you give a mental treatment, something happens. Every time you make an affirmation with conviction, something happens.

Expect results of your positive thinking immediately. Don't mentally wait for things to happen, but know that they are happening right now. The belief in delay or the belief that it takes time are obstructions that you must get out of your mind. When you speak your word, something has already taken place. This is why Jesus said the fields are "white already to harvest." The people around him said there were yet four months and then came the harvest. But Jesus said the fields were already white, meaning that the cause was recognized in Mind.

Before you plant, there is established in Mind just exactly what kind of a harvest you are going to reap. You decide what seed you will sow. Before you do anything, you come to a decision within your mind as to the kind and size of your crops. You have arrived at a conclusion. This is the way in which we use the creative principle. Before you give your treatment, you have a definite idea in mind. You know what your treatment is going to be, and you proceed to speak your treatment into form. You are simply putting into operation a law of Mind. Your treatment will manifest itself because that is the way in which the principle works.

You begin your mental creative work lots sooner than you are apt to realize. When you begin it, the creative cycle is already working. "Before they call, I will answer." The formal treatment represents the consummation in your mind of what you want. Realize that it is the action of the one Mind doing its perfect work now. Your treatment begins to act even before you consciously give it, for subconsciously you are always moving toward what you want.

Keep on the Path

IF YOU CREATE something you do not like, you can change it. What you create you can uncreate.

If conditions do not loosen their grip on you, perhaps you are not in your effective place. Consciousness establishes its own conditions. If things in your outer world are not moving fast enough, you need to clear your consciousness. Perhaps you are not doing what you really want to do and are trying to use will-power to make things happen. Don't try to go through the stone wall. Go back in consciousness. Change your idea; change your evaluation. Resistance, obstructions, and opposition could mean you are off your path.

Get still and let the new idea come through. Find yourself on your right path. Here things work smooothly, joyously, and powerfully. Stop struggling and forcing. "Not by might, nor by power, but by my spirit." Let God be you.

Great Expectations

YOUR THOUGHT IS a great creative power. What you think with conviction will become your experience. Your expectation and mental acceptance bring this about.

Expect to receive a greater good and prepare for it. Expect to be perfectly well and begin to accept the consciousness of health. Expect things to be better and richer. The action of subjective mind will fulfill your expectations.

This law can also work in a negative way. Expect to be slighted and ignored, and seldom will you be disappointed. Not because people go out of their way to hurt you but because subconsciously you have conditioned yourself to be slighted.

Change to the positive attitude. Expect friendliness and you will find friendliness. Expect to make sales, to have the right contacts, to be at the right place at the right time. Again, subconscious mind will justify your conviction.

Whatever you are seeking, expect to find it. Bring your conscious thinking and your subconscious acting together. Let each step carry the expectation of success. Whatever you do will be the outpicturing of your inner conviction.

Be Ready for
Your Demonstration

YOU CREATE YOUR opportunity in consciousness. Your design or pattern must be clear, and your direction must be unmistakable as you envision yourself fulfilling this design. Your visual power keeps your imagination constantly working until it becomes so real that you could almost reach out and touch it.

You prepare yourself to move into this new expression. When you have prepared yourself in consciousness and accepted your idea with your entire being, then you are ready. It is an inevitable consequence that consciousness makes itself manifest.

Your acceptance is a state of inner consciousness. Any delay would indicate your lack of acceptance; any opposition, interfering beliefs. You work on yourself. It is your awareness that must be made ready. You do not look to outside conditions, influences, or people. You ready yourself. Your inner acceptance knows when you are ready. Like the fruit falling from the tree when it is ripe, so your maturity or ripeness precipitates your opportunity.

Make Your Demonstration

PRINCIPLES ALWAYS WORK—whether you seem to use them or not. You have to grow into the consciousness of the idea you want to demonstrate. This is the only way you can use Principle.

The salesperson asks you to walk around the store until you grow accustomed to the new shoes. They must feel comfortable.

A new position or house may seem strange at first, and indeed it is until you grow into it. You put your thought in it and let your consciousness fill it.

The law of Mind objectifies what you think about, and you must be ready to accept your demonstration. You must be alert to act, just as when your number is called at the deli. You lose no time taking your place. It becomes your turn.

Do not forget what you are demonstrating. It will come. It cannot be delayed or stopped. Get ready for it. Put yourself into it. It is yours. Claim it and grow into it.

Take the Good

TODAY IS ALWAYS better than yesterday or tomorrow, for only today exists. You are the power of yesterday and the hope of tomorrow. But today you are the full awareness of Being. You can look in all directions but can actually see only what you are now and where you are now.

Nothing else is required of you—just being yourself where you are and knowing fully who you are. This is what makes life.

As the bee extracts only the honey and leaves the plant behind, so you take all of the good from every experience you've had and leave the experience behind. Each experience is complete. Perhaps more honey will tend to renew the contact—but only briefly. The past has gone.

You, the Self, remain the same. You function at the resurrection level—new hopes, new dreams, new ideals. Yet you find past, future, and present the same. Only your thought gives them life. The divine Self cannot be denied. Its integrity is forever. Its knowing opens the eyes.

Before the world was, I am.
Whither can they flee from thy presence?
I am that which was, is, and ever shall be.
I am the eternal resurrection.

Things Are Not Always What They Seem

YOU DO NOT understand an experience until you can explain its mental causes. Conditions are not always very important, but the ideas that precipitated them are. Causes are always invisible and hidden, but mental perception can ferret them out and bring them forth.

Each person's life is guided by his or her motives. To the selfish person, all experiences tend to cramp and restrict. To the unselfish person, experiences open up and flow out into a larger pattern of life.

To all appearances, each is finite. If each were his or her physical body, this would be true; but things are not always what they seem. You are mind and consciousness. Your thought goes forth and is felt by others, and you in turn are aware of what others are thinking about you. This invisible mind is the creative power.

What you really are is God in action, or Mind projecting itself. Therefore, your experiences reflect a state of consciousness. Build up attitudes of strength and success. Think in terms of self-sufficiency and power. In this way you act decisively. You inspire confidence in others because you have this inner conviction of your own stability. Establish a sense of authority within yourself that finds its expression in all of your relationships.

Your attitudes toward others reveal your basic attitude about yourself. Quarrelsome people are insecure; so are people who are gripped by competition. This appearance, however, is not a true reflection of what the person really is. It only shows how a person is thinking. You are where you are in life because of what you are in your thinking. Restrictive thinking can place you in restrictive positions. To change these conditions, change your thinking.

181

This changed thinking must operate on a level higher than that of the objective condition. The cause does not operate at the level of the effect. You cannot solve a problem at the level of the problem. Your thought must rise above the complexities and demands of the situation so that you can function without confusion. A chaotic condition does not mean the individual is chaotic except in his or her thinking. Don't be deceived by appearances. Nothing is happening to you and nothing has happened to your mind. You are that which used mind to think and to create. Make sure you see who you really are.

Learn to Discriminate

THE GREATER YOUR power of discrimination the greater your privilege of selecting what you desire. The more conscious of color you become, the more combinations of color become yours to use. The more discriminating your judgment and taste in music, the greater can be your repertoire of musical appreciation.

In like manner, the greater your understanding of the law of Mind, the greater your possibilities of using that law specifically. All thought is creative. Consequently, you will refrain from thinking that which you do not want to express. Do not allow to enter your consciousness those feelings which you do not want to assume form. What you think in secret, in the innermost depths of your being, shall be experienced openly in your world of form. There is no fear connected with this revelation, because of the joyous assurance that what you consciously choose to be *can* be through the law of Mind.

This discrimination opens an entire new world of creative thinking. It gives you the necessary concentration so that you can include the kind of harmony that you desire in your life. Your thought determines the degree of harmony. Your selectivity determines the harmonious expression that your life will assume. Choose the best way for your expression.

Principle Never Changes, but Your Experiences Do

EXPERIENCES COME AND go like the changing seasons, but the life principle never changes. Mind is the changeless creative power. Its thoughts and ideas may change, but its creative principle never varies.

Your sense of values changes when you change your point of view, but you can still be versatile. You can be many things to yourself as well as to your friends. The Science of Mind is a science at every level. You use the same Principle at work or at play. It can make you a good and safe driver, a great artist, a mighty financier. The Principle is the same; its different use gives it its variation. Fire can cook or burn, not knowing the difference. Ernest Holmes said that the thing that makes you sick is the same thing that can make you well.

Consciousness is the creative power, but you choose what you shall become through your use of it. You identify with what you see. You glory in the daffodils; their beauty is so great that you are not disturbed by their short duration. Then along come the azaleas, the marigolds, the petunias, and the roses. Each brings its particular brand of beauty.

But you have a creative principle behind all this succession of beautiful blossoms. You should enjoy the beauty but keep yourself identified with the Principle that created the beauty. That is the creative spirit of life. You enjoy the beauty of your home and environment. Your work gives you tremendous expansion of power. All of these, like the blossoms, are subject to change, but the life principle itself maintains a succession of positive, fulfilling experiences. You can identify with the spirit that is God. You are not concerned with changes in your outer expression because your consciousness is established in that Principle which can never be less than its perfect Being. This is the challenge to your thought.

Keep Growing

EVERY PERSON HAS the ability to grow. While physical growth may reach its peak, the mental and spiritual growth of each individual can continue forever. Life, as it unfolds from day to day, may repeat many experiences of your past. However, you can never meet a former situation in the same way—provided, of course, that you continue to grow.

Experiences *in themselves* cannot teach you anything; however, your reaction to each experience reflects your knowledge of yourself. You should constantly be working to increase your productivity and to enlarge your consciousness. This requires a conscious effort on your part. Your growth is not automatic, nor is there any guarantee of individual progress.

It is very apparent that many people take bypaths. Sometimes they let up on their vigilance or let discouragement cause them to slump. The evolutionary process permits you to take your time. You do not have to hurry or strain. You determine the speed of your progress. Your growth and spiritual unfoldment are in your hands.

Delays and procrastination are due to lack of confidence. Those who do not put forth the necessary effort toward success are dominated by their unbeliefs; their feelings of inadequacy have mesmerized them. Through the law of spiritual growth you increase your understanding. Mentally, you must keep yourself above every condition, at a higher level than the circumstances that surround you. When you learn not to be controlled by conditions, you can then create the conditions that you desire.

185

On Your Own

THE UNIVERSE IS founded upon a principle of Good. The fact that it is expanding and maintaining itself according to certain definite laws shows that there is a principle of coordination; otherwise you would have chaos, and it would not be long before the universe would self-destruct. This same principle is operative in you. The good in you is greater than your faults. You are stronger than your weaknesses. Your desire to cooperate and become a part of something greater than yourself outweighs any rebelliousness or eccentricity.

Every day affords you a greater opportunity to express good. Not that the day itself is good—the day has no power one way or the other. It's a good day when you make it that way. Every experience unfolds in the same way. Experiences are not things within themselves. They have no power for good or bad. But you have the power to make each experience good. The wisdom within you that knows how to make each experience work out in the right way is greater than any negative thinking.

The Bible says that when God created man, He called him very good. Because man was the embodiment of God's thought, God created His experience—which we call man—as He wanted him to be: in His own image and likeness. The good within you is not self-created. The Mind that created you made you that way. All good is within you because God put it there.